Momentary Buddhahood

Momentary Buddhahood

Mindfulness and the Vajrayana Path

by Anyen Rinpoche
Translated by Allison Graboski

Wisdom Publications • Boston

Wisdom Publications
199 Elm Street
Somerville MA 02144 USA
www.wisdompubs.org

Library of Congress Cataloging-in-Publication Data

Anyen Rinpoche.
 Momentary Buddhahood : mindfulness and the Vajrayana path / by Anyen Rinpoche ; translated by Allison Graboski.
    p. cm.
 ISBN 0-86171-598-5 (pbk. : alk. paper)
 1. Meditation—Tantric Buddhism. I. Graboski, Allison, 1974– II. Title.
 BQ8938.A68 2009
 294.3'925--dc22

                              2009009953

13 12 11 10 09
5 4 3 2 1

Cover design by Phil Pascuzzo. Interior design by Tony Lulek. Set in Bembo 12/17. Cover photography © Greg Cradick Photography.

Wisdom Publications' books are printed on acid-free paper and meet the guidelines for permanence and durability of the Production Guidelines for Book Longevity of the Council on Library Resources.

Printed in the United States of America.

This book was produced with environmental mindfulness. We have elected to print this title on 30% PCW recycled paper. As a result, we have saved the following resources: 14 trees, 4 million BTUs of energy, 1,286 lbs. of greenhouse gases, 6,193 gallons of water, and 376 lbs. of solid waste. For more information, please visit our website, www.wisdompubs.org. This paper is also FSC certified. For more information, please visit www.fscus.org.

Contents

Foreword

Mindfulness is the root of all the methods that tame
the mind.
First it focuses the mind. Then it eases the mind.
Finally it is the luminous nature, beyond thoughts.[1]

—*Patrul Rinpoche*

In Buddhist trainings, first you start by learning the teachings, then you enjoy the meditative experiences by practicing, and finally you reach the goal by realizing the truth: enlightenment. For success in such a journey, you must apply two indispensable factors, like the two feet required for walking. The first is the mindfulness (Tib., *dran pa;* Skt., *smr*) that keeps you on the path of training and drives you to the fruition. The second is the wisdom (Tib., *shes rab;* Skt., *prajna*) of knowing and realizing the stages of training and the goal, enlightenment.

Defining mindfulness, Asanga, the founder of the Yogachara school of Mahayana Buddhism, writes, "It is (a mental factor of) not forgetting (something) that is familiar to you and it is the action of not wavering (from it)." In this sentence, according to the celebrated scholar the Third Dodrupchen, Asanga clarifies three aspects of mindfulness: the never-forgetting aspect is the nature of mindfulness; the familiar aspect is the focus of mindfulness; not wavering from that focus aspect is the action of mindfulness.

1. *Thar pa'i them skas* by Shubham Shri Paltrul Sungbum, Folio10a/5, Vol. Ka. (Tibet: Dzogchen Edition).

Some of those who are new to Buddhism might think that meditation on mindfulness belongs solely to the tradition of breathing meditations. And mindfulness of breathing is indeed an important training of "calm abiding" (Tib., *zhi gnas;* Skt., *shamatha*) and also of "insight" (Tib., *lhag mthong;* Skt., *vipashyana*) meditation traditions. In calm abiding, you focus your mind one pointedly on your breathing or on a mental object. In insight, you see the nature of the breathing or the object, as it is. However, the meditations of mindfulness and wisdom, or calm abiding and insight, are not limited to the breathing meditations. In fact, they can be found in almost every kind and level of Buddhist training.

First, they train you to fully focus your mind toward the right direction. Whether you are a Buddhist or a non-believer, a meditator or a worldly person—all these methods can make your life healthier and meaningful by cultivating and cherishing some degree of mindfulness, the most precious quality of your own mind. You cultivate mindfulness by calmly focusing your mind, one pointedly, on Buddhist or positive secular images, sounds, feelings, thoughts, or actions and by staying away from indulging in any unhealthy chains of wild goose–chasing thoughts or actions.

If you are focusing your mind on any healthy and beneficial object and action with total mindfulness and enjoying it fully, then every step of your action will take you along the right path of securing happiness, peace, and wisdom—without any sidetracks.

If you lack mindfulness, then even in your daily chores, you frequently forget to finish half the things on your to do list. You often say or do things without thinking beforehand and regret them later, when your life and relationships are falling apart as

the result. It is such a pain! You may know lots of Dharma teachings, but are unable to apply any to enhance your life. It is such
a waste. You do enjoy some good experiences while meditating,
but as soon as you get out of the room, they all go out the win-
dow. So hopeless! You sit for hours in a meditation posture, but
your wild mind restlessly wanders all over the world. Such a joke!
You have spent years doing some meditation, but there is little
gain as your mind never engaged in it fully. It is such a failure! You
have so many gifts and such capacity, but very little has even been
realized and utilized. Such a pity. You are facing all these disap-
pointments and much more, through the fault of a single culprit:
lack of mindfulness.

If you could build the habit of mindfulness in your mental
stream by training in focusing your mind fully and earnestly on
whatever you are feeling or doing, then even if you are just saying a simple prayer or feeling loving-kindness for a few minutes,
since you are doing it wholeheartedly and enjoying it with a fully
opened mind, its effects will be vivid, powerful, and long lasting.

In order to improve your daily life and especially your meditation, it is essential for you to train and tame the wild elephant-
like mind by tying it with the rope of mindfulness. With an alert
mind and healthy intention, you must engage with whatever you
are thinking or doing with undivided attention. If your mind is
distracted, just keep bringing it back on track, again and again.
The great bodhisattva Shantideva writes,

> If the elephant-like mind is tied to (positive thoughts)
> With the rope of mindfulness,
> All the dangers will disappear and
> All the virtues will come into your hands.

What's more, mindfulness eases the grip of grasping of the mind, opens it to all the infinite fields of wisdom, and secures it as the vast treasure of memory.

Whatever Buddhist meditation you pursue, it will always possess two indispensable components: mindfulness and wisdom. For example, when you are meditating on loving-kindness, you might be able to remain in the thought or feeling of loving-kindness without distraction. If so, that is mindfulness and your ability to maintain it is because of mindfulness. In the same way, if you are meditating on a visualized image—the aspect of focusing and stabilizing your mind with the details of the visualized image precisely and calmly—that is mindfulness and your ability to maintain it is because of mindfulness. The aspect of realizing, experiencing, or being aware of peacefulness, boundlessness, emptiness, or openness—the true qualities or true nature of the visualized image or loving-kindness, as it is—is wisdom.

Some extraordinary meditations and attainments of mindfulness are also taught in the teachings on memory (Tib., *gzung;* Skt., *dharani*). Through mindfulness and wisdom, highly accomplished bodhisattvas meditate on and realize the four never-forgetting memories (Tib., *mi brjed pa'i gzungs*), namely: the never-forgetting memory of the words of Dharma (Tib., *chos gzungs*); the never-forgetting memory of their meaning (Tib., *don gzungs*); the never-forgetting memory of the esoteric mantras (Tib., *sngags gzungs*) that serve others; and the never-forgetting memory of forbearance or confidence (Tib., *bzod gzungs*). In the memory of forbearance, bodhisattvas, by using the sign of a consonant or vowel such as the letter/sound *Ah*, which is known as the door of emptiness, vividly remember infinite words and meanings and their emptiness nature. Because of the interdependent causation of using such a syllable with mindfulness and wisdom, the memory of space-like boundless wisdom of emptiness nature opens, and the memory of infinite words and meanings will then be awakened or perfected. Also, the memory of infinite words and meanings, in turn, expands or perfects the realization of the wisdom of the emptiness nature. Thus each activates the other, like a bicycle's two wheels, to lead to the goal.

The ultimate goal of meditation on mindfulness is the realization of the spontaneously present union of mindfulness and wisdom that is non-dual, enlightened, timeless, and boundless.

According to Dzogchen teachings, if the essential attainments are achieved, if you watch the *rigpa* (intrinsic awareness, the true nature of the mind) with your relative mindfulness, directly and nakedly, without grasping at it or conceptualizing it, soon your relative mindfulness will unite with the *rigpa*. For the true nature of the absolute mindfulness and of the ultimate wisdom is inseparable union. The absolute mindfulness is always present naturally in our own *rigpa* and we realize it by uniting our relative mindfulness with it through meditation.

The third Dodrupchen explains:

> If you maintain the unmodified *rigpa* nakedly, the mindfulness
> that was the maintainer will merge with the vast expanse of
> *rigpa* that has been maintained, like salt melting into water.

Mindfulness is the most powerful and essential training of all that can turn every movement of our thoughts and every activity of our lives into something positive. Mindfulness drives us along the right path and opens us to infinite treasures of bodhisattva qualities. It unites us with the ultimate goal, the luminous union of mindfulness and wisdom—with buddhahood.

With his brilliant scholarship in Buddhism and intimate knowledge of the minds of both East and West, Anyen Rinpoche has produced a truly insightful guidebook on mindfulness, a precious gift for Dharma students, new and old alike. I trust that by taking in these nectar-like teachings of Buddhism, we can rejuvenate the mindfulness that is inherent in us all.

Tulku Thondup Rinpoche

The Buddhayana Foundation, USA

Dedication

I dedicate this book to the memory of my supreme root master:

For eons, though a completely manifest buddha, you
    came to the ordinary world
again and again in the form of a spiritual master.
The captain of beings in the degenerate time, Tsara
    Dharmakirti:
from my heart I remember your kindness; please keep
    me within yours.

Your excellent teachings are the essential nectar
    whose flavor is liberation;
Upon tasting it, the fever of the three poisons is
    completely pacified.

In order to benefit others, I composed this supreme
    path of mindfulness and discernment of the sutra
    and tantra
in accordance with your own experience and spoken
    words.
It was excellently arranged without altering your
    essential meaning.

Whoever takes up these teachings properly
will have no difficulty in attaining liberation in the
   primordial, vast expanse.

Thus, based on the proper reliance upon and practice of
the effortful path of mindfulness and discernment,
the supreme, effortless, mindfulness of suchness of
   Atiyoga will arise naturally, spontaneously,
and free of contrivance.

Gratefully dedicated to Tsara Dharmakirti Rinpoche

Acknowledgments

I would also like to acknowledge the indispensible help of Allison Graboski in preparing this book, as well as all of my other students who contributed their time to preparing it: Jody Luna, Julie Benson, Bea Ferrigno, Eileen Cahoon, Phil Williams, and Spencer Ames. Finally, I would like to thank Josh Bartok and everyone at Wisdom Publications for all of their hard work getting it prepared for publication.

Editor's Preface

This book is based on talks given by Anyen Rinpoche in 2005–2006, one year after he arrived in America. Though he had been working with Westerners for only a short time, he had already seen certain common gaps in our understanding of the Buddhist path in general, and especially in American's understanding of the Vajrayana path. Some of the students he met were quite experienced and had been studying the Buddhist path for years and others were new to the path, yet the gaps in their understanding were mainly the same.

One of the prevalent misconceptions among Western Vajrayana Buddhists is that the tradition of mindfulness is somehow a Zen or Theravada Buddhist teaching, and is not essential for tantric practice. Anyen Rinpoche was adamant that all Vajrayana practitioners should fully understand the crucial support that mindfulness brings to the practice of tantric meditation and especially to meditation that is free of all reference points, also known in the Tibetan tradition as Dzogchen or Mahamudra. Without the foundation mindfulness provides, it is impossible to realize the pith of these beneficial and profound forms of practice.

Another misconception is the usual Western understanding of the term "mindfulness" itself. Through question-and-answer sessions with students, Anyen Rinpoche realized that the practice of mindfulness has been understood too narrowly, and many students had missed the true depth and meaning of this type of mind training. Without making the connection between mindfulness and Vajrayana, a rare opportunity to gain experience in the profound tantric tradition is lost. With this in mind, Anyen Rinpoche embarked on a full year of teaching to clarify the confusion on this subject; we have created the present book from his talks and discussions with American students.

May it dispel the dark clouds of ignorance that obscure the naturally radiant minds of beings everywhere; may it enable all beings to joyfully engage in mind training as a support for the complete realization of the path!

Allison Graboski

CHAPTER I

Mindfulness and Discernment Defined

The omniscient master Longchenpa said:

> Mindfulness is like an excellent hook
> That grasps the wild, untrained elephant of the mind
> It completely reverses fault [so that one] naturally
>   enters virtue,
> From this moment, the mind should rely upon it.
>
> Discernment is like an undistracted, excellent night
>   watchman.
> The thief of non-virtue cannot find an opportunity to
>   steal
> The many gems of virtue, which it protects.
> From this moment, one should certainly rely upon it.

When speaking of a bodhisattva's conduct—one who has dedicated her- or himself to the path of awakening in the service of all beings—we refer to outer conduct, expressed through the body and speech. Yet even more important than these is the quality of the mind, for the mind determines the conduct of the body and speech. We could even say that the mind is the king of the body and speech. No matter what aspect of practice we are talking about—whether it is view, meditation, or conduct—all of it is reliant on the mind.

Spiritual practitioners who wish to attain mastery over the mind should have deep familiarity with the two conditions that make such mental mastery possible, namely mindfulness and discernment. The reason that I chose to write an entire book on this topic is because I assume that each person who enters the Buddhist path wants to become an excellent meditation practitioner. If you want to become an excellent meditation practitioner, I want to give you the tools to do it. I want to tell you frankly and openly what you need to know, so that you are empowered to take your practice into your own hands.

Whenever we are reflecting on how mindfulness fits into other types of ritual practices, we have to keep in mind that the exact way the Vajrayana teachings are practiced usually varies from student to student. Although the essence of the teachings remains the same, the methods can be individualized. Because each student is developing an understanding of how to practice meditation in a way that is attuned to his or her specific personality and habitual patterns, developing a relationship with a spiritual friend, a lama, is crucial in our tradition. Without the lama, who can help us see ourselves from the outside and guide us along the path, we will have no idea how to use the variety of methods in the Vajrayana tradition. To truly master the whole of Vajrayana mindfulness—outer, inner, and secret mindfulness—we must rely upon a spiritual friend. I will discuss this more in depth in chapter 5.

Understanding Mindfulness and Discernment

To take a step back for a moment, I want to point out that "mindfulness" is often translated as a singular term in English. However, in the Tibetan language it is usually accompanied by the word "discernment," and the two create a compound word. In Tibetan, the word we use is *dren shey*, which literally means "mindfulness and discernment"—but it is translated into English only as "mindfulness."

The first syllable, *dren,* can be understood to be a variant of the the verb "to remember." It points to the quality of remembering or keeping something in the mind. The second syllable, *shey,* can be translated as "discernment" or "introspection." It has the implication of knowing, and describes the quality of being aware of what is happening in the mind, so that we know when we need to apply the other tools of practice. Thus, the synchronization of these two qualities makes meditation on the teachings of both sutra and tantra possible.

Before we proceed let me now say a few words about those two terms. Sutra and tantra are two distinct types of teachings in the Buddhist tradition. The texts called sutra explain the outer Buddhist teachings and are suitable for the majority of practitioners. The teachings of the tantra are the inner and secret Buddhist teachings, which give extraordinary methods and rely on heightened skill, devotion, and aptitude to be put into practice. We will further explore the relation between these two throughout this text.

Through introspection, we notice the mind's momentary agitation, and then we remember what it is we are to practice. However, it is the synthesis of noticing and remembering that enables us to refine whichever practice we are cultivating. Generally, this refers to entering into meditation without falling into any extremes. The mind is neither wild nor dull. Each of the components of *dren shey* has its own quality in relation to meditation, so I use the terms *mindfulness* and *discernment* specifically to point out those distinct functions of the mind.

To summarize, mindfulness or remembering is what ties the mind up and discernment is what analyzes or observes or tries to decide, "Is this conduct virtuous? Is this action of body or speech skillful? Am I doing the appropriate thing for this exact moment?" Another way to describe this is to say that the quality of mindfulness enables us to remember our lama's instructions and the quality of discernment enables us to know how and in what situations to apply them. We can really only separate discernment and mindfulness in a very subtle way, in order to help us understand their complementary aspects. Ordinarily, we would not notice the difference between them at all.

These two qualities help transform us into authentic practitioners and support our progress toward realization. It was said by the great master Shantideva, "Except for taming the mind, there is no reason to work at taming." In other words, without subduing the mind, there is little value in practicing meditation. Furthermore, there is no practice as potent at taming the mind as training in mindfulness and discernment.

Conventional and Ultimate Reality

As a foundational matter, whenever we are talking about Buddhist philosophy, and specifically whenever we are talking about the mind, we must always distinguish between *conventional* and *ultimate* reality. Conventional reality is perceived as a result of the ordinary mind's instinctual grasping. For example, the mind mistakenly grasps what is impure as pure, what is suffering as happiness, and what is impermanent as permanent. This mistake, or impure perception, is the root of the truth of conventional reality. Many of us practitioners know that the nature of samsara is suffering and that we should not grasp on to phenomena that are fleeting and momentary—yet even though we know this, we are powerless to perceive them any other way. This is a result of our strong investment in, belief in, and grasping at conventional reality.

In contrast, ultimately the "three spheres" of the perceiver, the object, and the interaction between them are *empty*—there is no object to grasp, no one grasping, and no action of grasping. This is the truth of ultimate reality. Recently, a very experienced student asked me about the word *emptiness*. Why do we use such a word, and what does it point out to us linguistically? This is a good question.

Ordinarily, we always think of the world around us, of all beings and phenomena, as being either existent or nonexistent. Again, this is the way we perceive things conventionally. Referring to such perceptions and phenomena as "empty" points out that there is something beyond these extremes of existence and nonexistence. When the teachings say that beings and phenomena are empty, they remind us of the need to overcome the mind's tendency to ally emptiness with nonexistence. But emptiness is completely beyond any conventional mode of being. For that reason, the recognition and experience of emptiness is part of the second of the two truths, the truth of ultimate reality.

Additionally, *emptiness* is a word we use to describe the true nature of phenomena. When we thoroughly investigate any being or phenomena to see if there is a lasting, inherently existent unchanging nature present, we will always have to conclude that there is not. And we express this by saying that the being or phenomenon is "empty."

We cannot mix the two truths when we are analyzing the nature of phenomena. If we mix them, thinking that conventionally everything is empty and therefore inconsequential, we will lose all respect for our ordinary world. We will make grave mistakes such as thinking that uncompassionate or nonvirtuous conduct is without implication and that the law of karma does not exist; that how we act, speak, or think doesn't matter. We will become deluded into thinking that we do not even need to practice meditation because, after all, ultimately all things are empty and of the nature of completely perfected wisdom. This would be a grave error indeed!

For that reason, we must always make sure which of the two truths applies when we are talking. For example, when we are talking about the empty nature of beings and phenomena, we are within the realm of ultimate reality. Likewise, if we are talking about any ordinary worldly interaction, we are within the realm of conventional reality.

For ordinary beings, the experiences of ultimate and conventional reality are distinct, while a buddha experiences no distinction. Since a buddha's wisdom is completely omniscient, the way a buddha perceives is beyond our ordinary, conventional understanding. We should keep this in mind as we read this book and particularly as the teachings progress from those on sutras to those of the tantras.

The mind in its ultimate sense is described in the sutras, the outer teachings, as being free of any defining characteristics. This means it has no color, shape, texture, or any other fixed quality. Rather, the mind's nature is luminosity. However, this description is not very helpful when we are starting out on the path of meditation, trying to get to know and relate to the "kitchen-sink" mind, the ordinary mind that helps us get through our day-to-day lives.

There are some profound yet simple metaphors that describe mindfulness and discernment in the Vajrayana tradition. To understand more clearly how mindfulness and discernment work, first take the traditional example of the mind as a wild elephant. A wild elephant is the perfect example of the mind, because of its massive energy, and its hugely destructive potential. Because we are aware of the wild elephant's tendencies, we would never leave it alone in the town square (for instance), unwatched and unchecked.

If we were attempting to tame the elephant, we would tie the elephant with a rope so that we could lead it. That would be mindfulness. The actual tamer of the elephant, who continually notices the elephant's behavior, would be discernment. We can see that if either mindfulness or discernment were missing, taming the mind would not be possible.

Using our metaphor, what is the consequence of not having either the rope or the tamer present when working with the elephant? If we are missing the tamer—discernment—no matter what the mind is doing, no matter which kind of afflictive emotion it is generating, there is nobody looking out for it, and nobody to notice what has happened. As a result, the mind does whatever it wants. On the other hand, even if we have discernment and we have no mindfulness, we see the mind's discursiveness, but we do not have the mental stability that enables us to bring the mind back under our control. We have no method for that. In both cases the wild elephant of the mind will run around and do whatever it wants—knocking down trees perhaps, and maybe stomping on unsuspecting harmless creatures!

Another way to describe the relationship between mindfulness and discernment is by using the metaphor of climbing up a very steep and dangerous mountain. If we had both eyes to rely upon, we would have a much better chance of making it safely to the top of that mountain. If for some reason one eye or the other were closed or blinded, it would be very hard for us to make it safely to the top. Mindfulness and discernment are like those two eyes that are constantly and vigilantly watching over our meditation, providing complementary perspectives—like the left and right eye—that together make sure we can find and grab on to sure and safe footing, all the way up that steep mountain.

Method and Wisdom

We must have a method and a way to work with ultimate reality because it so completely transcends our ordinary experience. To realize the ultimate nature of mind, we rely upon examples from the scriptures, metaphors, and conventional methods for working with the mind. In our Vajrayana tradition, many conventional methods are used to help us develop mind stability, or *shamatha*. For example, reciting mantras softly or through song and the visualization of sacred syllables and forms are both simple ways that can be used to help the mind focus and develop stability. That is the purpose of the two types of accumulations in the Buddhist path:

the accumulations of method and wisdom. By relying on method, we can transcend ordinary mind and relate directly to wisdom. So, both method and wisdom are essential to realization.

Mindfulness and discernment, as we will see, relate to both the method and wisdom aspects of the path. In the beginning, they are the methods for calming and taming the mind. Later on the path, they become the mechanisms by which self-liberation of concepts and afflictions and abiding in the nature of mind, presented in the teachings on Dzogchen or Mahamudra, are possible. Dzogchen and Mahamudra are supreme teachings that are given to students who have trained in the outer and inner teachings of the Vajrayana path, have supreme devotion in a qualified lama, and have developed extraordinary mindfulness and discernment. The term "self-liberation of concepts" implies that any concept or afflictive emotion can be freed "right on the spot," effortlessly, through the mastery of these secret transmissions.

One method that practitioners on the bodhisattva path use to realize the ultimate nature of mind is that of the six *paramitas,* literally translated as "the practices that take us to the far shores of samsara." The paramitas are six good qualities that a bodhisattva must develop in order to benefit beings and attain complete realization. These six are: generosity, discipline, patience, joyful exertion or diligence, meditative concentration, and wisdom. Additionally, by training in any one of the paramitas, it is possible to realize all six because to perfect one requires a perfection of the other five. We can understand the six paramitas in the context of the two accumulations. The first five are classified as method, and the last as wisdom. The perfection of the six paramitas is simply another way of describing the perfection of the two accumulations, or the perfection of method and wisdom.

However, even a teaching like the six paramitas cannot be practiced without mindfulness and discernment. If we lack these two qualities when we take up the six paramitas, we wind up doing a lot of contradictory things. At the outset we might imagine "I am practicing generosity" or one of the other paramitas, but what actually happens is that, because we do not have proper mindfulness and discernment, we will easily fail to carry out our intention. We actually have good motivation when we start—and good motivation is very important—but when we carry out the action, we do it wrong. For example, we might start out with the good intention to help a family member who is ill by taking care of him or her. In the beginning, we have a motivation of generosity and loving-kindness toward that being. However, impatience may arise while we are taking care of him or her. We may become tired or irritated because of the effort we are making, or because we do not feel appreciated. If we do not notice that we are irritated, and then, upon noticing, renew our initial motivation, then our conduct has become at odds with our initial purpose. Thus, mindfulness and discernment enable us to reconcile our motivation with our conduct, or harness our energy on the path.

Momentary Buddhahood

Mindfulness and discernment are even present in a fully realized buddha, although the way buddhas express these qualities is different than that of ordinary beings. One way to describe a buddha is to say that the buddha's mind continually expresses the nature of wisdom. From our point of view, a buddha can meditate at all times and under any circumstances. It does not matter what activity the buddha engages in, nothing impairs or obscures the buddha's realization. If we had to ask what quality of mind enables the buddha to meditate in every situation, the answer must be that it is the perfection and mastery of mindfulness and discernment. Because the buddha has perfected these qualities, they are effortlessly expressed.

The perfection of mindfulness and discernment are necessary for the continual expression of wisdom that is experienced when abiding in the nature of mind, free of distraction. In the final chapter of this book, we will discuss "the mindfulness and discernment of *suchness.*" This is the complete mastery of mindfulness and discernment, imbued with the primordially pure view of Dzogchen and Mahamudra. In other words, mindfulness and discernment are spontaneously present and perfected in wisdom itself.

Mindfulness and discernment become like a bridge between the ordinary mind and ordinary practice, and realization. As we begin to master mindfulness and discernment, we discover that the experience of enlightenment is possible at each moment. This is not meant to be a mere intellectual exercise; by engaging in serious mind training, we can actually experience glimpses of enlightenment through the practice of meditation free from all reference points. This is what I call "momentary buddhahood."

Generally, we think of enlightenment as something that happens all at once, like a tidal wave that cleans everything impure away. However, this is not actually how realization happens. Realization happens *incrementally,* from moment to moment. In the moment when perfect wisdom is recognized and all concepts and afflictions are freed right on the spot, a practitioner can experience something similar to a moment of buddhahood. We will explore this tantalizing idea more in the final chapter of this book.

Other Ways to Understand Mindfulness and Discernment

Take a moment to reflect quickly on the different places your mind has gone since you got up this morning. So far today, my mind already went to Tibet and back. I have remembered some things that happened in the past, such as meeting the Dalai Lama in India, sitting having breakfast with my root lama in Tibet, and watching a beautiful, silent snowstorm in the late fall. The mind can travel all over the world in a matter of seconds. Your mind may have left the room you are in right now, just since you began reading this chapter. Maybe you thought about your parents, your son or daughter, your husband or wife, or what you will do at work tomorrow. Even though we might sit down and take some time to reflect on the Dharma, we still are not able to maintain our focus. Why is that? It is because the mind lacks mindfulness and discernment, so we cannot focus one pointedly on anything. The phrase "one pointedness" describes the mind's ability, based on mindfulness and discernment, to be completely absorbed or focused, and free of distraction.

The word *mindfulness*—in the sense of "remembering"—can be understood nicely in relation to the spiritual friend. The reason I bring this up is that earlier, I talked about practicing the six paramitas and having contradictions come up in our practice. When we rely on a spiritual friend, he or she gives us some methods to resolve these contradictions. By remembering the spiritual friend's instructions, transformation becomes possible.

An even better definition of mindfulness, which stems from this, is "keep the mind constantly focused on virtue." So, the thing that the mind remembers, the thing the mind is mindful *of,* is virtuous conduct. Remembering our aspiration toward virtuous conduct is what enables each of us to be able to work steadily toward it.

There are people who will inevitably ask, "Can't I practice mindfulness without relying on a spiritual friend, on a lama or guru?" I would suggest that for ordinary people, for most of us, it is very difficult first of all to see the contradictions in our behavior, our motivation, and our conduct. And then it is even more difficult to know how to resolve those things. A genuine spiritual friend will have a lot of insight into the student's behavior. As the relationship deepens, it is often very easy for a spiritual friend to suggest how a student can unify his or her conduct and aspiration.

There is one more useful way we can describe the word *mindfulness,* which is as a synonym of "remembrance." For example, if we are relying upon a spiritual friend who gives us oral instructions—profound instructions on subtle practices that we should practice for the rest of our lives—but we fail to keep up our practice, we obviously will not master what is being taught. However, if we have strong faith in our spiritual friend, I believe that at the time of death the quality of our faith will give rise to mindfulness, and we will remember our spiritual friend's instructions. This is another way to understand the quality of remembering as one of the supreme supports to meditation.

Mindfulness and discernment also keep us from generating and accumulating bad karma, negative habits of mind and body whose imprints lead to the creation of more suffering. Perhaps we have a spiritual friend with whom we have a close relationship. If we do, that spiritual friend is probably always pointing out our faults because that is what spiritual friends do to their beloved students—they help us become aware of and change our deeply ingrained habits. However, the directness and honesty of a kind-hearted spiritual friend is very hard to bear without getting agitated. Perhaps it's something small, like our teacher telling us that our posture is wrong, or something larger, like our attitude and approach to life and practice need work. We are ordinary beings and the minute we hear something we do not like, the mind starts to generate all kinds of negativity.

In my own relationship with my lama, I was heavily criticized. In front of an audience of two or three people, my lama often said that I was arrogant. Especially because this was true, it was not pleasant to hear. If I had known in my heart it were not true, it would probably not have bothered me so much. However, I always relied upon mindfulness and discernment to immediately reflect on my own faults, and vow to correct them. Thus, my lama's criticism became a wonderful opportunity for mindfulness training. In sum, even though we may want to accept our teacher's words, we may, at this time, lack the patience to tolerate them.

And yet if we have developed strong mindfulness and discernment, we will already be aware of the faults our teacher is pointing out because, hopefully, we will have begun to see these faults arising—not just the fruits and consequences of them having arisen. Mindfulness and discernment are like very clear eyes that we can see through. We do not have to be shocked by our teacher's words, because the mind constantly discloses our imperfections to us. In truth, each of us knows ourselves better than anyone else does. Deep down inside, we know when we are doing something wrong or against our own values—if not at that moment, we at least know it at some point after the fact. If we have mindfulness and discernment, we also have the ability to correct or purify any wrongdoing we may have committed. We are always fully empowered to change. We do not have to rely on someone outside of us to tell us that our conduct or attitude is wrong. We do not have to get angry or frustrated at them for noticing; and we need not be embarrassed or ashamed. With the tools of mindfulness and discernment, we can really take notice of ourselves in a way that might have seemed impossible before.

By relating to the spiritual friend, a practitioner learns mindfulness and discernment as well as a variety of methods to practice meditation. Based on that, we can begin to act as our own teacher by recognizing both our good qualities and, realistically, our faults. And then, as we do, we can apply mindfulness and discernment as much as possible to further perfect our conduct. If we develop strong faith in our teacher and the Dharma instructions we have been given, our training—supported by faith—will allow us to remember those instructions and apply them in every moment, throughout our lives and even up to the moment of death.

Mindfulness and Discernment as Part of Daily Practice

It would be good for all of us to start practicing mindfulness and discernment on a daily basis. But I want to be clear that the mindfulness and discernment I speak of is not only a sitting practice, not just something to be done a few minutes a day in a special place. It is an engaged practice, too. When we are on our cushions, we should notice when the mind strays. As soon as we do, we simply begin our meditation again.

Students often ask what is meant by the phrase "begin your meditation again." I admit, it does sound cryptic. However, it is a phrase that can only be understood by doing. Really it just means bringing the mind back and beginning whatever practice or technique you have been working with. If you are visualizing, you refresh the visualization and begin again. If you are reciting mantra or noticing the breath, you renew your effort and begin again.

When we notice the mind is generating, because of conditioning and past habits, any sort of negativity, we should instead turn our mind to generating bodhichitta and loving-kindness for ourselves as well as all beings who are suffering. Bodhichitta can be defined as the aspiration to remain in samsara until all beings have been liberated from suffering, and, it should be noted that to do this requires that we master the method and wisdom of the path as well. Not just on the cushion, but also in our daily lives, we should generate bodhichitta any time the mind feels agitated or afflicted. Based on this simple tool of mind training, recalling our aspiration that all beings be free from suffering, we will start to notice whenever our conduct is at odds with our motivation. More importantly, we will notice when we *lose* our bodhichitta, our compassionate heart, and our patience with ourselves or others. As we become aware of what is happening in the mind, we can make a renewed effort to practice the instructions we have learned or been taught, to purify the mind, and take steps toward a definite change. This too is the practice of mindfulness and discernment.

Mindfulness and discernment are important from both the dharmic point of view and the worldly point of view. Needless to say, if we do not cultivate mindfulness and discernment, we are not going to be able to meditate—it is just not going to happen. Also, if we try to perform any other kind of dharmic activity, the action will wind up being done impurely. Again, this is because the action will not be based on the perfect aspiration that inspired the activity.

In our worldly lives, trying to do our jobs or interact with people without mindfulness and discernment will not work optimally either. We can really think of the teachings on mindfulness and discernment as a life skill—not only a Dharma skill. They are abilities we can use in every area of our lives and relationships, and are beneficial to everyone.

Linking Mindfulness and Vajrayana

We should not fall into the trap of thinking that mindfulness teachings are only about *outer* conduct and only important at the *beginning* of the path. As we will see in the later chapters of this book, mindfulness and discernment are crucial for advanced Vajrayana practitioners and beginners alike. What if at this moment Milarepa, a great realized master, came and gave us oral instructions on how to realize the nature of mind? That would be really wonderful. But what if we lacked mindfulness and discernment? On the one hand, it's good to receive these instructions, but on the other hand we have to be prepared to receive them and put them into action. This is something that we are going to be reflecting on throughout this text.

Taking this idea a little further, if we have already received oral instructions on how to realize the nature of mind, then we have been given the method to practice. Even in this case, if we lack mindfulness and discernment, one of two things will happen. First, we may have an afflictive emotion and because we lack mindfulness, we will forget to practice. For example, we may have received instructions on how to self-liberate afflictions, but when we get angry, we are overpowered by our anger and fail to notice that we are angry until the energy has amplified and become strong.

Or, without discernment, we will remember that we are supposed to practice but we will not have any idea how to do it. Instead, the mind will be blank and we will think, "What am I supposed to do in this situation right now?" Both are a common experience when we are overwhelmed by strong afflictive emotions. Without mindfulness and discernment, receiving instructions that teach how to realize the nature of mind and not receiving the instructions have the same result: we are not able to practice them.

I have heard Dharma students claim that if we know the primordially pure view of Dzogchen and Mahamudra, we do not need anything else. But, even if having the view is like the heart of meditation practice, remember that a heart cannot exist in isolation. A heart is part of a body, and relies upon the overall body system to make it function correctly. The body supports the heart, and vice versa. Mindfulness and discernment support the heart of our meditation and also bring our meditation to life and sustain it.

For example, we tend to externalize the enemies of the mind— for instance, we open our windows and get irritated because somebody outside is making too much noise. Or somebody says something to us that we do not like and we wish they would stop. I have even heard of students being irritated by the sound of household appliances when they are meditating! We are always thinking about the things around us that we wish we could change in order to feel better. It is mastery over mindfulness and discernment that causes these things not to be perceived as enemies anymore, that enables us to truly transform them to conditions for practice and abiding in the primordially pure view.

Mindfulness and discernment pacify all outer and inner enemies of the practice of meditation because they are what make meditation possible in each moment. When we are emotionally overwhelmed, as we usually are, meditation is not possible because the mind is distracted. And yet even just noticing the mind's distraction is what causes the mind to open up and creates an opportunity to meditate.

No matter what part of the path we are working on right now, if we have the qualities of mindfulness and discernment, we will be empowered to improve our meditation. This is not particularly a beginning instruction; it is not particularly an advanced instruction. It is a type of instruction that is applicable to each and every individual's practice.

It was said by the great master Shantideva that:

> Reciting prayers and mantras and taking up ascetic
>   conduct
> Even if done for long periods of time
> While the mind is distracted
> Are said to have no purpose at all.

Without the qualities of mindfulness and discernment to help make sure our practice is purposeful and has the proper motivation, we can actually make great effort without getting a good result.

It was also said by the master Sakya Pandita, a great and ancient realized master of the Sakya lineage, that mindfulness and discernment are necessary to "bind the wild elephant of the mind to the pillar of virtue." Without binding the wild elephant to the pillar of virtue, we find it difficult to take adverse or even pleasurable conditions to the path. Although we like the idea of making our whole lives our spiritual practice, we ordinary beings find it impossible to truly incorporate Dharma into our daily lives without relying on mindfulness and discernment. Instead, we often deceive ourselves into thinking that we are practicing constantly, when actually most of our lives are passing by unwatched and unexamined.

What would the mind be like without mindfulness and discernment? Think of the metaphor of the waves on the ocean, or the blowing wind—always in motion, never steady. Any attempt to practice *shamatha,* calm abiding meditation, or tantric meditation free of all reference points, would fail for lack of stability.

Usually, concepts move over the mind like waves on the ocean. Maybe we are thinking about the past, remembering something that we liked or did not like. Maybe we are thinking about the future and something that we hope will happen or hope will not happen. Or maybe we are thinking about right now and things that are dissatisfying or satisfying; things that we want to happen; things that we wish we were doing right now. Reflecting on this ever-shifting quality of the mind, we can see how crucial mind stability is for a practitioner.

One final thing to reflect on is what the conduct of a retreat yogi is like. Perhaps you have never had the chance to be around a Tibetan yogi who has been in lifelong retreat or who has at least been in retreat for many, many years. As you will see, this is a topic I enjoy talking about not only because of the magical quality that realized masters express, but also because of the very practical example they set for us. The quality of such beings is very different. The way that they talk, the way they walk, the way they eat—everything about them feels different. I would say that this difference results from the skill with which they bring mindfulness and discernment into all of their activities.

Additionally, we should know with certainty that any great yogi in history such as Longchenpa, Jigme Lingpa, Tilopa, or Naropa relied upon mindfulness and discernment to realize the nature of mind. Based on that, they were liberated from the constraints of the five elements. It was said they could change water into fire and fire into water. But the otherworldly abilities they developed started out as training in ordinary mindfulness and discernment. It was based on this ordinary training that the experience of meditation became possible on a momentary basis, and extraordinary experience blossomed.

If we do not realize the nature of mind and then master it, whether we like it or not, we will remain subject to the suffering of the three realms, we will experience all of the different dynamics of afflicted emotions, and the non-virtue that we accumulate will certainly ripen into suffering.

As we stated above, the method for taming the wild elephant of the mind is through mindfulness and discernment. It was said by Master Atisha that when one is able to subdue the mind, all outer enemies, objects of impatience, sources of anger, and sensory objects that inspire attachment cease to agitate the mind. In contrast, when we do not tame the mind and lack mindfulness and discernment, anything the mind attaches to, or feels impatient or angry with, becomes very powerful within the mind. Such events or objects agitate and distress the mind, and cause us to obsess. It is like the inner enemy of ordinary mind is setting us on fire; the inner enemy of ordinary mind is ruining us; the inner enemy of the mind is spoiling the good things we have to express and the good we want to do for ourselves and others. As Atisha instructed, "Reflect on this power that the agitated mind has over you and work to develop mindfulness and discernment."

Summary

Two supreme methods to train in mindfulness were presented in this chapter:

When doing sitting meditation, notice when the mind is distracted, renew your initial effort and motivation, and "begin your practice again" as often as necessary.

In your daily life, examine your motivation using bodhichitta as a guidepost. Renew your aspiration to act from bodhichitta as a way to bring your conduct in line with your highest motivation.

CHAPTER 2

Mindful Motivation and Speech

It is good to keep in mind that if we only develop mindfulness and discernment as outer qualities that are
detached from the mind, we could become inauthentic in our
relationships with others. In other words, we might present a certain face to the world and behave in a certain way, but really in
our hearts we do not mean it. In my experience, this has happened to many people who are born into Asian cultures, who
train from childhood in mindfulness and discernment, but not
necessarily meditation. And I have seen this both in my culture
and elsewhere.

I lived in Japan for several years. Japan is a beautiful county that
has a strong Buddhist culture. Many people in the West are familiar with the Japanese Zen tradition, which is of course a tradition
that emphasizes mindfulness. There have been a lot of great Buddhist practitioners in Japan throughout the ages, but Japan's religious culture has changed in the modern era. Now, most people
are not religious. People teach their children and grandchildren
that "work is religion." However, there are still Buddhist values
and instructions remaining within the culture; for example, being
mindful of others' feelings, and acting and speaking carefully to
create harmony and good will with others around you. This is a
very wonderful thing to be part of. People act very kindly toward

one another, and are extremely careful not to let each other feel out of place.

The downside is that often Japanese people exemplify mixing mindfulness and discernment with outer conduct only. While there, I felt that I did not truly know if the person before me would do what he or she said or not, because he or she might be speaking only to preserve harmony.

It is common for people of any culture, really, to stumble: people may say one thing to your face but do another when you are out of sight.

This is not caused by a lack of goodwill. Rather, the situation is more that many people have Buddhist ideas but do not meditate. They do not take up all the aspects of mindfulness exactly the way they are supposed to be taken up. So they are only working with part of the instruction—that of the outer conduct, and that leads to inauthenticity. Outer conduct and aspiration still have to be brought together, and this can only be done through taking up an authentic meditation practice.

We cannot fault or judge others for the way they are raised or for their culture or beliefs or attitudes; we can only learn from them and apply what we see to ourselves. Each and every one of us has the potential to twist a practice of mindfulness into a way to make ourselves look good, or to make others like us—and this can happen even if we initially start out with a pure aspiration. So we must be vigilant that our aspiration remains pure, or that it returns again and again to wholesomeness.

We may meet someone who says that he or she has been a practitioner for a very long time. This person may seem like a practitioner because his or her conduct seems outwardly very good, very in line with the Dharma. But in fact, that person may never have applied mindfulness to the mind; he or she may have only applied it to his or her outer conduct. This person's talk about the Dharma might be lip service. This is a danger for all of us. When we see it in ourselves, we must recognize that this is mere self-attachment. Even well-intentioned practitioners can allow their own minds to deceive them, and make them honestly believe that they are something that they are not. This is something that every Dharma practitioner is susceptible to, so we each have to be careful not to fall into such a habit.

It could also happen that we become overwhelmingly deceptive through paying so much attention to our body and speech. We could become the kind of person that no one could ever intimately know because we are always trying to please others. We are always so outwardly focused that we never let anyone else in. A Tibetan proverb says, "Speech is like a lamb's fleece, while the mind is like a vat of poison." The kind of person exemplified by this proverb is soft on the outside, where everything looks good, but on the inside there has been no fundamental change and the person is as filled with greed, anger, and ignorance as ever. This definitely will not help us on the path; we should avoid developing this attitude at all costs.

Please understand that I mean to caution against the extremes of both sides. On one hand, being too direct, as we often are in the West, can hurt people. Sometimes "brutal" honesty is not warranted under the circumstances. But on the other hand, being totally soft and just telling people what they want to hear is not bodhisattva conduct either. I am advocating a kind of conduct that falls into neither extreme. In order to avoid extremes, we need mindfulness and discernment to help us be aware of what we are thinking, doing, and saying.

Affecting the Mind

When our practice of meditation is consistent, it has an effect on the mind. This naturally causes our speech to be transformed; it naturally brings the attitude of bodhichitta into our speech. However, in the beginning we have to make a lot of effort. If we are strong practitioners of meditation, we will be less in the grip of strong afflictive emotions and our own strong opinions.

One of the reasons I am focusing so much on purifying our speech as a way to really affect and transform the mind is that speech holds a great power over others. It is often the case that people remember what we say far longer than we ourselves do. Speech has the power to heal and the power to hurt. We should remember this the next time we speak without thinking at all. One simple way we can truly embody the bodhisattva's way of life is just by simply taking a moment to reflect on what we wish to say.

Additionally, the great master Sakya Pandita described practitioners who focus only on conduct as being like tadpoles, because they have big heads, big mouths, and they are very hungry. In the beginning, they cannot get enough, but their stomachs are much smaller than their mouths. They cannot hold anything inside, they have no way to get big and strong. This is another way of saying that sometimes we are too serious and too eager in the beginning for our energy to be sustainable.

Truly, we must strive from the beginning to transform actions of body, speech, and mind together. We should try to digest everything we learn. And when we do, we will naturally be nourished and transformed by teachings, becoming strong of mind and skillful and effective in action and word, instead of remaining skinny, small, and weak.

Examining Motivations

Oftentimes when we read the Buddhist teachings, it seems like worldly things are somehow corrupted or bad, and that only Dharma is a pure activity. But actually it is not like that. Everything has to do with the individual who is practicing Dharma. If our practice is pure and proper, then we do not have to choose between good and bad, worldly and dharmic.

Even if we think we are taking up the practice of Dharma, if we lack mindfulness and discernment, our Dharma practice will become something else, something that is not Dharma. We have to be really careful not to let that happen. Perhaps even using the word "Dharma" is inaccurate because each person has his or her own concept of what Dharma is.

With this in mind, whenever we are sitting down to meditate or we are going to receive a teaching, it is important to take a moment and, using our mindfulness and discernment, examine ourselves as well as the person whose teaching we are receiving. We should make sure that our motivation is pure, that we are really clear on what we are doing and what our intent is. We should not let our hunger for teachings blind us to our own motivations or justify failing to examine the teacher from whom we are receiving teachings. Mindfulness and discernment are our vehicles for examining ourselves and others. We should not make quick, impulsive decisions about the teachings that we study and the teachers who guide us.

We should take the time to examine a lama before we undertake serious study with him or her. What kind of connection do we feel with the lama personally? What kind of study has that lama undertaken, and what kind of conduct does he or she keep? Is the lama's own conduct an expression of the meaning of the teachings, and does it express authentic bodhichitta?

In terms of developing a relationship with a spiritual friend, we need to take the time to get to know each other. This does not happen overnight. We have to build trust and reveal our character to one another so we know how to work together. This is especially important in a tradition like ours, where each practitioner is working with a spiritual guide to develop a practice that suits him or her perfectly. Additionally, if we get in the habit of examining ourselves and others now, we will become more skillful at this as time goes on, and will know how to make proper choices that are in our best interests as practitioners.

No matter what activity we take up, the first thing to do is reflect on and examine our motivation. If it is not the virtuous motivation of bodhichitta, then we should work to release whatever afflictive emotion has caught our mind. This could be done by reflecting on the impermanence of the situation, or on the dissatisfactory nature of samsara, which is always full of suffering, as well as any other method we have been taught by our spiritual friend. As long as we do that, we have at least laid the foundation for pure activity. This is how we actually do bring bodhichitta into our actions.

Say we are out in the world and something is bothering us. We feel like saying something about it. If we are not sure of our motivation for speaking, it might often be a better choice to say nothing at all. It might be better to be quiet and reflect on why we were going to say a particular thing, on what our subtle motivations are, and whether we are acting from grasping, aversion, or selfishness. Alternately, we could try to clarify our motivation for speaking so that we can do our best to make sure that our words will have a harmonious effect or truly be in the interest of others. But this is rarely how we approach our speech, isn't it? Sometimes we speak because we just want to "get something off of our chest" without any thought for how the person we are addressing might perceive what we have to say. Sometimes we just want to make ourselves feel better, and we do not think about whether there is someone else with whom it would be better to share particular thoughts and feelings. We should balance our own needs with those of others and we should not be selfish in our need to express ourselves.

Another option in this situation is to meditate on the view or to practice *tonglen,* the compassion practice of "sending and receiving." Tonglen is a method by which we take on the suffering of others and send them our happiness, thereby counteracting the mind's natural narcissistic tendencies. Many people react strongly to hearing a description of this practice, fearing that they will actually take on another's "negative energy." To assuage such fears, I will say right now that it is not possible for us ordinary practitioners to directly take on such energy—the practice is merely metaphoric. However, through this practice, we can transform the impulse to speak into the experience of meditation by using it to purify our own motivation. Whatever we do, it is good to remember that all kinds of thoughts come up in the mind, and if we are not tempering them with mindfulness and discernment we might say or do something we will regret.

Because we all have a lot of self-attachment, it is very easy for our motivation to become corrupted. For example, some of us may be practicing prostrations as part of *ngondro,* or foundational practice. Before we begin prostrating, we should think to ourselves, "Why am I doing this prostration right now? Am I doing it because I believe it's deepening my practice and my foundation in meditation? Am I doing it because I have an aspiration of bodhichitta and I wish all beings to be free from suffering? Am I doing it because I think that I will be able to receive an incredible tantric initiation after I am done?" It is easy for our practice to become utilitarian, so to speak, done in order to attain a specific thing. On the other hand, sometimes our practice becomes rote, done out of habit and no particularly clear motivation at all. If we get into the habit of examining our motivation and being mindful about it, we will notice when our motivation has been corrupted and we will be able to purify it. Nobody's motivation is pure all of the time. The trick is seeing the difference, and having the chance to correct it—and this is precisely what the practices of mindfulness and discernment provide.

The practice of ngondro, for instance, is important in developing skills in faith, pure perception, diligence, visualization, one-pointedness, and concentration. But if we are practicing ngondro simply as a bargaining chip to use with our teacher or to impress others, then practicing ngondro, though perhaps still somewhat valuable, will not be life-changing for us. How sad! The way to allow the practice to truly be life-changing is to check in on our mind, and be sure that, on a daily basis, on a moment-to-moment basis, we are practicing for the right reason.

Many people practice Dharma to feel happy or more at peace, and they find that sometimes meditation helps them feel that way. But if this is the reason we practice, we will not be transformed by our practice because our motivation is not proper. When this is the case, we will only find a certain inconsistent and temporary kind of happiness, instead of true liberation. When we practice with the motivation to just feel at peace, we may be able to sit quietly—in other words, perform the outer conduct of a practitioner—but this is not the same as taming the mind. However, if we are really working on mindfulness and discernment, we will notice a gradual change in the mind. Nagarjuna, one of the great Buddhist scholars of this age, said, "Just as the moon waxes, good qualities should increase day by day." It is obvious that Nagarjuna's instructions depend on mindfulness and discernment.

The text I am reflecting on as background for these teachings is Shantideva's *Entering the Way of a Bodhisattva*. One of the reasons the title uses the word "entering" is because conduct follows after the mind, and hopefully enters the mind at some point—so that they become completely indivisible. The great master Shantideva lived the meaning of all of his teachings. For example, he vowed that he would never let his mind be distracted. When he said this, Shantideva wasn't talking about *vinaya*, or monastic conduct, he was simply talking about his sitting practice and his mind during daily life. When our eyes are not on the mind, they are looking around for something to get attached to. When our eyes are constantly on the mind, we have less opportunity to get caught up in our afflictive emotions.

Shantideva also said that, no matter what we are doing, we should have the gaze of meditative absorption. This refers to *shamatha* practice, and how our eyes are open and our gaze goes over the top of the nose so we can only see a few feet in front of us. This helps us to stay focused on our practice when we are sitting. We can take this same instruction into our daily lives, although it becomes more of a metaphoric kind of instruction.

The very first time I received teachings on *Entering the Way of the Bodhisattva,* there was one member of my sangha, another monk, who was taking all the instructions very literally. He was actually a little extreme about it. One day, he received the instruction about keeping the eyes gazing across the top of the nose. He tried to practice the instruction in his daily life, as he was walking. The hermitage where we were studying was in the middle of a forest and one afternoon the monk went the wrong way on the path. Unknowingly, he wandered into the forest and slammed his head into a tree!

We have to remember these are instructions to benefit the mind—they are not exact directions for every circumstance. We should not latch on to them so strongly that we think the outer conduct is the most important part. The inner experience is the important part. The outer conduct only helps us get there. The monk received a nickname that meant, "Do not pretend to be something you are not." His name reminded all of us of that important lesson.

If we make the words of a teaching more important than its meaning, we become judgmental of others and our application of the teachings becomes a basis for arrogance. That is why the Buddha Shakyamuni said, "Between the words and the meaning, pay attention to the meaning." This statement is why we put so much importance on motivation in the Buddhist tradition. Whenever we fail to notice our motivation, we are in danger of hurting or harming others through either our actions or our attitude. Again, it is important to be honest and make an honest effort.

Commitment

Before a bodhisattva makes any kind of commitment or promise, he or she must exercise caution. A bodhisattva does not make promises without first using mindfulness and discernment to examine and ensure that he or she can follow through on that commitment. This refers to both practice commitments as well as worldly commitments. In our modern lives, there are many new things we can see and try out. Things happen so quickly that it is very easy constantly to have new ideas about what we want to do. It is very important to think through this aspect of bodhisattva conduct and take up commitments mindfully, knowing what we are getting ourselves into before we commit.

The logic behind this, of course, is that if we make a commitment in one area of our lives and we are able to follow through on that commitment, it becomes easier to follow through on other commitments. If we commit to walking three miles each day to improve our health but then start to skip days because we feel too tired or unmotivated, over time, we will lose our ability to keep that commitment. The next time we want to make a commitment, we will be under the shadow of our previously unkept promise. It will undermine our confidence and cause us to feel that we are not capable of following through. We must be vigilant of this pattern and strive to keep it from arising; once it has arisen, we need to strive to break free from it.

When we apply this idea to meditation—even if we are only planning to take up a practice for a limited period of time—once we complete that practice it becomes easier to take up and complete other practices in the future. That creates a positive condition for us to develop our practice. It gives us self-confidence and a real sense that we are capable of being genuine practitioners. This is part of how we uphold the bodhisattva vow.

Let us take a moment to think about what this vow entails. The bodhisattva vow is a promise we make not just for this lifetime, but for all of our future lifetimes. We vow we are going to keep working at realizing wisdom for the benefit of all the count-less beings who are suffering until samsara is completely empty of suffering beings. If we cannot keep even a simple commitment in this present lifetime, it is difficult to imagine that we could keep our bodhisattva vow, which entails so much endurance and hard-ship sustained over such a vast period of time. But each time we keep any commitment at all, whether our sacred commitments to our spiritual teacher or ordinary commitments, we are strength-ening our ability to uphold our bodhisattva vow. This is just another way of taking our ordinary life conditions and using them as an extraordinary support for realization.

I have met my fair share of people who have started a serious practice like *ngondro* multiple times, but have never even finished it once. The reason why this happens is because we take on new projects, commitments, and responsibilities without thinking. We do not take the time to actually think through how it is we are going to keep the commitments we have already made. It is very easy for one commitment to interrupt another, and the result is that we are not even able to finish one thing; we cannot even learn to do one practice well.

This tendency of the mind is illustrated by the traditional metaphor of a monkey walking through a cornfield. Every time the monkey sees a new ear of corn, it wants to pick it up. So what happens each time it picks up an ear of corn? It has to drop one that it is already holding. If we act this way toward our medita-tion, we are going to find that our meditation does not improve. This is really self-defeating. We have to be careful not to act like the monkey in the cornfield.

One scripture gives us sound advice on this topic:

If a new task is taken up before a prior one is complete
Neither of them will be accomplished, it is simply
  exhausting!
When walking, place one foot in front of the other.
Moving both at the same time will cause you to fall
  down.

Not Being Attached

There is a story about two of the Buddha Shakyamuni's close students, Shariputra and Maudgalyayana, who—before they became his disciples and took monastic vows—went to the equivalent of some kind of bar or brothel where people were listening to music, drinking, and watching beautiful women dance. When they were young, they were famous scholars, though not of the Buddhist tradition. Later, of course, they would go on to have many students and be brilliant Dharma practitioners. Both of them had good dispositions for Dharma practice; they had natural tendencies toward modesty, and toward mindfulness and discernment.

And so at this ancient brothel, it quickly became apparent to them that they were quite different from the others gathered there. They had come to this place to please their friends and family, but while they were there they watched their minds with extreme care. The people nearby thought they were foolish because they did not seem to be engaging at all with the atmosphere around them. They were both reflecting on the situation as a mere appearance, with no true existence. As they were talking together, one said to the other, "My ears can hear and my eyes can see, but I am not attached to the sights and sounds around me as though they were substantially real."

Just like these two people, we are never going to exist in a world that we do not see and we do not hear. We are never going to be able to simply shut out the world and cut ourselves off from everything. But even though sights and sounds appear, we can still meditate. We can still practice Dharma, using this story as an example. The only difference between someone who can do what Shariputra and Maudgalyayana did and someone who cannot is the ability to focus the mind, and practice mindfulness and discernment.

Just as Tilopa said to his heart son Naropa, "Son, appearances do not bind us, we are bound by attachments. Cut through attachment." Abandon your investment in worldly things; abandon your attachment! But make no mistake—the idea behind Dharma practice is not to stop relating to the world.

The Bodhisattva in Samsara

We have to take some time to reflect on what it means to be a practitioner on the bodhisattva path. If we think, "I am a bodhisattva and I am going to abandon samsara and go somewhere else," we have made two mistakes. First of all, there is no escape. There is nowhere else to go. And second of all, a bodhisattva is not thinking about *escaping* from samsara, or getting to any particular state at all. A bodhisattva is simply thinking about *reengaging* in samsara and practicing for the benefit of others.

We can also consider the kinds of situations that we face on a daily basis as we try to gain insight into how we are to work with the Buddhist path. We must engage with other people in the world. But, for example, when someone is talking to us, if we do not fall into an extreme by generating attachment or anger toward what that person is saying, then we are not accumulating a lot of bad karma based on the interaction. The kind of karma we accumulate is totally dependent on the conditions in the mind and how we relate to whatever is happening.

If we could somehow escape and cut ourselves off from the world, and find a place where we did not have to see or hear any of the worldly interactions that distract us, we would still find that the mind is as noisy and untamed as ever. Simply avoiding worldly places will not subdue the monkey mind. Isolating ourselves from the rest of the world does not magically endow us with the ability to meditate. Instead, we should consider what is happening in the mind. If our conceptual thoughts and habitual tendencies are what seem to give us trouble, we have to deal with those first. Mindfulness and discernment are the primary ways to work with the ordinary mind and the bombardment of conceptual thoughts that arise.

Reflect on the idea that if the mind were free of conceptual thoughts, then no matter what we saw or what we heard, none of it could bother us. Always come back to reflecting on what is happening in the mind.

Whether we are sitting down or engaging in work, eating, sleeping, or walking, we should constantly look at the three doors of body, speech, and mind and be aware of what is happening with them. This is really how a bodhisattva trains; this is how a bodhisattva becomes a realized being. If we have a fantasy that being a bodhisattva or a great master of meditation means that we can leave samsara behind and escape this world for a more pristine environment, we will be disillusioned by Dharma practice.

Truly speaking, who causes samsara and nirvana to be different? We do that. Our ordinary, dualistic minds do that. And who unifies samsara and nirvana, so that the experiences of samsara are just like walking through a beautiful garden? That could be us, too, if we focused on training in bodhisattva conduct.

Summary

Four topics for mindful reflection:

Reflect on what you plan to say before you say it. Why are you speaking? Are you avoiding the extremes of brutal honesty and inauthenticity?

Examine your motivation before you sit down to practice or listen to a Dharma teaching. Is your motivation that of authentic bodhichitta or is it worldly and utilitarian?

Examine potential commitments before you undertake them. Do you feel certain you can complete a task or practice before you undertake it?

Examine your motivation about the bodhisattva path. At any given moment, are you practicing with a motivation to merely escape samsara?

CHAPTER 3

Mindfulness Day and Night

When we understand the benefit of mind training, it helps us gain enthusiasm and motivation to practice day and night.

When I teach on mindfulness and discernment, I generally focus on speech and, of course, the mind, but I do not often talk much about the conduct of the body. I will just say a few things about that now.

In general, it is said that a bodhisattva is always careful and cautious whenever taking action. We talked about this in the previous chapter, in terms of making commitments. But this also refers to all our actions, generally. No matter what it is we are doing, whether we are standing up or lying down or in the midst of placing our cushion on the floor, all of our actions should be done with precision and care.

It is also said that any representation of the body, speech, or mind of the buddhas—meaning any Dharma texts, meditation seats or cushions, prayers, paintings, statues, or offerings—should be treated with respect. Dharma practitioners practicing mindfully do not place such items on the floor unless that is the item's natural place, such as a cushion. We do not step over them. We do not put things on top of them. We are thoughtful and conscientious when we handle them. We could think that this is a very arbitrary rule—but this is not actually the purpose of the instruction.

Actually, this is an ingenious instruction that points out how it is possible for each and every practitioner to develop faith and cultivate a relationship with the essence of the teachings by expressing respect toward sacred objects. This is a way to remind ourselves that our Dharma practice is something new we are bringing to our ordinary lives. Additionally, this is a way to start to see Buddhism and the supports for our practice as being truly sacred; we honor them when we handle them, and we treat them respectfully. I think this is one of the reasons we do rituals in the first place—it is through rituals that practices start to become part of our lives and we start to relate to them as having their own special energies and good qualities.

A ritual is something we do the same way each time because of the energy it invokes through its doing. In our tradition, many ritual practices such as *tsok* or *yidam* practice have been passed down directly from master to student for generations. When a master realizes a ritual practice, the practice is taught precisely so that the student may practice in the same way, and the same experience will result.

Additionally, when we do a ritual practice, we must understand how to bring together the practice, including any gesture or mudra or ritual objects, and the mind itself. A spiritual friend can instruct us on how to use all of these good conditions in our practice. Rituals do not work when done inauthentically. If we do not develop a true feeling that practice and ritual objects are sacred, they will not yield results. When we keep a ritual practice at arm's length and do not get to know it intimately, it will never become powerful for us personally; it will only ever be something that someone else relied upon and found useful. If we develop devotion and trust in the ritual, recognizing that it has the potential to lead us, too, to realization, then a ritual becomes truly blessed and powerful for us personally.

Another part of making ritual practice sacred is through developing what Vajrayana Buddhism calls "pure perception." Pure perception in its authentic form is the genuine perception of a realized being, one who sees all beings and phenomena as expressions of wisdom. Even though we ordinary beings do not see worldly objects and beings purely now, we must train with the idea that they actually are perfect expressions of wisdom even though we can not see that. This creates a new habitual tendency, which predisposes us to being able to recognize ultimate reality. The idea is that if we treat ordinary objects as having sacred qualities, and being authentic expressions of wisdom, we can one day see even what we may have thought of as ordinary objects— things made of brass, stone, clay, or canvas—as having the same ultimate nature as the Buddha's wisdom.

One reason that in my teaching I do not place a lot of importance on the conduct of the body is because this seems to be a place where we can become confused about realization and the development of good qualities. As we discussed in the previous chapter, sometimes people may act as real masters of outer conduct so that when we see them we think, "That is a great person." We have reflected on the fact that this may or may not be true. However, it is all too easy to get caught up in appearances and forget that the quality of each person's mind is fundamentally more important.

My reason for focusing on the conduct of the mind more than the conduct of the body comes from an experience I had in Tibet, which probably applies universally. I already mentioned that when I was about seventeen, I studied Shantideva's text for the first time with my root lama. There were about twenty monks gathered together to undertake this course of study. At that time, we were not allowed to gather as large groups to study and practice Dharma, so our group was small. My lama told us that everybody needed to adhere to the outer conduct that was laid out in the text and focus on having virtuous conduct of body and speech.

Overnight, one of the monks in the group became like a saint. He was able to put all the instructions into practice seemingly perfectly, and people praised him and looked up to him. But strictly on instinct, I was not sure that his conduct was going to last. Somebody mentioned the monk's superior conduct to me, and I said, "We will see in a year or two. If he has really changed, it will be obvious to us in the future that he has made a genuine, lasting change. We will all know that he truly transformed his mind." My own personality tends to be quite cautious and open, so I usually wait and see what people show me over time rather than make quick judgments.

Sadly, after a year or two, this monk gave up his vows, started drinking and began slaughtering animals for a living. I learned from this experience that even someone who is very serious about Dharma practice at one point can later get caught up in the wrong things because he or she did not understand how to practice properly in the beginning. This is one reason why I teach with a constant focus on the mind as the root of conduct for the body and speech.

Mindfulness Gone Astray

It is important to note that mindfulness, in and of itself, is not always an inherent good. There are examples of mindful conduct in nature that show us that not all mindful actions are compassionate actions. Take the example of a hawk flying over a great body of water, looking to catch a fish. The hawk has to fly very slowly, evenly, and mindfully because he does not want to scare the fish away. If he is not mindful, he will not get what he wants. Immediately upon discerning the presence of his prey, he changes his course and attacks.

Another example is that of a cat stalking a bird. That cat has to be very mindful and have the utmost control over its body in order to pounce on the bird. Think about the cat's inner motivation, and how different that is from what we presume to be the good qualities of mindful outer activity.

If we were thieves trying to break into a house, we could do it if we were very quiet and careful as we crept inside. Once we did that, we could look around for what we wanted. We would find that if we were noisy or unmindful, we would not be skillful thieves.

Needless to say, this metaphor points out what our Dharma practice should not become. Mindfulness is very important, but we must always remember that the mind is the root of everything expressed through the body and speech. Although we have to make effort at disciplining all three aspects of body, speech, and mind, the main focus must remain on the mind. The motivation in the mind must be pure for the karma of mindfulness to be wholesome.

Bringing Mindfulness into Sleep

We can practice mindfulness each night as we prepare to go to sleep by using the following instructions.

The posture we should fall asleep in is the one the Buddha Shakyamuni used when he passed into nirvana, which is called the lion's posture. A demonstration of that posture can be found in images of the Buddha passing into nirvana, if you would like to take a look.

Let me elucidate a few details about this posture: the right hand should be placed underneath the right cheek, so that the upper body is propped up. The space between the crook of the arm and the head should be such that a two-year-old child would be able to climb through the crook of the arm. That might be a little bit difficult and strenuous—but that is the traditional instruction. Alternatively, if that posture is not suited to our body, we can allow ourselves to simply lie with the right

side of the head on top of the right arm, with the elbow folded so that the right hand can be placed beneath the right cheek. The legs should be stacked one on top of the other and the left hand should be on the hip.

There are four reasons given for using this posture while sleeping, and reflecting on them can help us be inspired to actually make the effort to fall asleep in this posture.

The first reason is that, when we actually have some kind of discipline or posture while sleeping, it creates a good condition for continual training throughout our entire life, and subsequent lifetimes too. If we neglect to practice at night, and only focus on the daytime, we can get messy or sloppy because we are not being careful consistently and continually. By now it should be apparent that *consistency* in the mind is the hallmark of meditation, mindfulness, and shamatha, and is what generally creates the conditions for mental stability.

The second good quality of sleeping in this posture is that it creates a good condition for us to one day be able to practice, for example, dream yoga while we sleep. It enables us to bring the energy of meditation and prayer into our sleep.

The third reason to practice this posture is because if we try to bring mindfulness into our sleep without the posture, our sleep will be very thick and heavy. In other words, we might have the tendency to just kind of slip off into ignorance or bewilderment while we are sleeping instead of bringing the quality of mindfulness into our sleep and our dreams.

The final reason is that it helps us not to have non-virtuous thoughts or dreams because the posture brings the energy of mindfulness to the activity of sleeping. In turn, this helps us not to accumulate non-virtue during the night.

The instruction I have just given is only about the body's physical posture. We have not yet talked about the mind or any motivational component at all. So let us turn our attention to those latter details.

Of course we ordinary practitioners do not have the same capacity as do lifelong retreatants, monks, and nuns who renounce the world to practice continually. The kind of aspiration that a lifelong retreatant has before he or she falls asleep might be a merely virtuous motivation, but more likely this kind of yogi would either have the motivation to rest, or would actually be resting, *in the very nature of mind which is primordial, pristine wisdom.* He or she would also think, "As much as possible, I am committed to making an effort to rest in the nature of mind while I am awake or asleep, as often as possible. I will continue increasing my efforts and maintaining diligence toward that end until my sleeping life and my waking life become one and the same—until I am able to practice under any and all circumstances."

I suggest that we also reflect on words such as these before falling asleep. My own root lama told me that if I had this motivation before I went to sleep, I would at least have a dream with insightful signs, and that my dreams would benefit my practice. He also said if I were really fortunate and diligent, I would be able to abide in the nature of mind as well. Even if we are not at this point in our meditation abilities, and do not yet have the ability to rest in the pure nature of the mind, there will still be some benefit or positive conditions created while we are sleeping.

Patrul Rinpoche gave an alternate way to work with the mind as we fall asleep: focus on a bright light—perhaps imagining some kind of luminosity appearing before our eyes—and then fall asleep engaged in that visualization. But do please note: imagination is not synonymous with visualization in the Vajrayana teachings. Patrul Rinpoche said that falling asleep while focusing the mind on a bright light would enable a practitioner to bring the quality of luminosity and meditation into the sleep state. And yet, if we try this for the first time—and maybe even the twentieth, fortieth, or hundredth time as well—we will probably find that it wakes us up rather than puts us to sleep. But if we work at it slowly, over time we will learn how to calm the rush of wind energy that this kind of visualization arouses in the upper part of the body. I will talk more about working with wind energy in chapter 7.

It may be hard to imagine falling asleep while abiding in the nature of mind or experiencing luminosity in the dream state, but we can work on cultivating the conditions for this to happen by using the simple techniques I have just described, even if no results are immediately apparent or we feel we have little success.

Patrul Rinpoche gave one final instruction to be used before falling asleep: If we cannot, at this time, focus on a light or abide in luminosity while we fall asleep, we can reflect on the *four immeasurables* instead. The four immeasurables are a type of mind training in which a practitioner attempts to cultivate and express the mind's potential for immeasureable equanimity, loving-kindness, compassion, and rejoicing in the happiness, good fortune, and merit of all sentient beings. By reflecting on the four immeasurables regularly before falling asleep, eventually we will be able to reflect on them while sleeping because the mind will become habituated to that reflection. Patrul Rinpoche said that when we reach the point that our remembrance and practice of the four immeasurables in our waking lives is equal to our practice of the four immeasurables while we are sleeping, we will

finally be prepared to recognize luminosity in the dream state—
and to extend mindfulness and discernment into every moment
of our lives, waking or sleeping.

Summary

Four ways to train in mindfulness through conduct:

Train the body in mindful conduct, paying special attention
to conduct around ritual practice and ritual items.

Train the mind in seeing ritual items and practice as being
sacred and different from other material objects and actions
in daily life as a basis for developing pure perception.

Reflect on the connection between mindfulness and outer
conduct.

Train in mindfulness through posture and an appropriate
technique when falling asleep as presented in this chapter.

CHAPTER 4

Bringing Mindfulness
into the Three Spheres

All beings possess the same nature and potential to experience wisdom as the buddhas do. This is what we call buddha nature. Supposing that we all have that innate nature of wisdom—the same nature of a buddha—we might think to ourselves, then, why are we all abiding in samsara and experiencing suffering? The first answer is very simple, of course: we suffer because of ignorance. We experience ignorance in all the different ways the mind grasps. The second answer is that the supports for meditation, for direct experience of ultimate reality, including mindfulness and discernment, are lacking. So again, we flounder in samsara.

We have spent considerable time talking about mindfulness and discernment as ways to know ourselves and our own motivation, and as ways to keep an eye on our own inner and outer conduct. At this point we might wonder what main elements we should focus on when we sit down to practice, and how mindfulness and discernment would support them.

To answer this question, it would be good to first reflect on ignorance and the confusion we experience as ordinary beings. The actual condition of confusion has three elements, which are called the three spheres. First, there is the sphere of dualistic mind that perceives. Second, there is the sphere of the object being perceived. And, third, there is the sphere of the action occurring between them. Sometimes this action can be more of a mental concept or interaction, as well.

We all have five sense faculties, or five doors of consciousness. Even though we may have learned that all phenomena are "empty" and know from a philosophical point of view that things have no inherent true existence, the mind still believes that the things around us are real based on what it learns from the five senses. Our only way to relate to sensory objects is to grasp them mentally or physically. This is how the perceiver, the object, and the perception create the situation of dualistic confusion.

Mindfulness and discernment, if we have trained properly, can help us realize that all appearances in the ordinary conventional world are based upon confusion. Imagine what we would be like if we did not believe that the things around us were truly existent. We might see something beautiful or experience something we did not like, but because we did not believe it was truly existent, it would not have the same power over us. For example, we might have strong attachment toward a particular type of delicious food. However, if we reflect on the food as being a mere appearance, we will not have the same visceral experience even when we see or smell that food. Likewise, this would be true if we reflected on an enemy as not being truly existent. If we met our enemy, his or her attitude and energy would not affect us the same way as if we felt a strong investment in the situation. Thus, by reflecting on the emptiness of the three spheres, we would not have the same aversion or anger toward a situation that we did not like, or the same desire for something we really wanted or thought was wonderful.

Remember the story of Shariputra and Maudgalyayana? Their mindfulness and discernment were strong enough to support them even in a situation that would completely overpower the senses of an ordinary person. That is what made them the incredible practitioners we still talk about today.

The Thirty-Seven Practices of a Bodhisattva says:

> Like apprehending a beautiful, charming object
> Like summertime, when everything is
>   rainbow-colored
> Having the view that nothing is truly existent, just a
>   gorgeous appearance
> And abandoning all attachment is the practice of a
>   bodhisattva.

This quotation comes from the point of view of how we relate to one of the three spheres: the object. If we properly understand the object, then we will neither become attached to nor feel any aversion toward it. At first, this happens intellectually, as merely an intellectual exercise. When we notice that attachment or aversion have arisen, we reflect on the fact that all phenomena are like a dream or an illusion. However, when we use this kind of reflection as a reference point for training in mindfulness over a long period of time, it begins to transcend mere intellectualism. As we move deeper into the Vajrayana path, it is possible for this to become a genuine experience.

Next, examine the perceiver, the person whose mind is grasping. When we reflect on our own self-attachment, it is easy to see that self-attachment creates the condition of suffering that causes us to feel a lot of pain and anxiety about things around us. When we grasp at the self as being truly existent, this causes us to relate to our world in a certain way and causes us suffering. Part of our training is that every time we notice that we are experiencing self-grasping, we reflect on the fact that the self is impermanent. We can use whatever method we prefer to reflect on the self's impermanence or emptiness.

We have examined the object itself and the apprehending mind, now we should also think about the conceptualization that happens when a person's mind apprehends an object. Again, that conceptual thought or afflictive emotion, whatever experience it may be, also causes us to experience samsara if we are not able to recognize it as the Dharmakaya, which is a term that is synonymous with the nature of mind or indivisible wisdom itself. That causes us to accumulate karma and to experience suffering. I will talk more about recognizing momentary experience as the Dharmakaya in chapter 8.

Instantaneous Expression

When we analyze how the things we experience in our daily lives truly arise, we can see that they all arise co-emergently. This is to say that they arise instantaneously, from moment to moment. "Co-emergent" also refers to the fact that when phenomena manifest instantaneously, there is no first and second arising, no now and later. Although we normally apprehend conventional reality as a continuous chain of events, actually reality manifests from moment to moment like a magical display.

When we grasp the experiences in our ordinary, busy lives, it appears that one thing builds upon another, that things are permanent and lasting, so that our lives are based on solidity and continuity. We do not have the perspective that things are actually arising moment by moment and then passing away. In other words, things appear but are empty. We do not realize that birth, death, and rebirth are actually with us each and every moment.

Ultimately, all appearances that arise—even just in the ordinary world around us—arise from the nature of mind. But we usually do not clearly know what the nature of mind is, nor do most of us understand how to abide in the nature of mind. Because of this, the mind's natural expression, which is primordial wisdom, becomes an expression of confusion that we grasp at simply because we do not understand how to work with it in any other way. Again, the problem of grasping is one of repeated habit, and a lack of insight about how to change the way the mind functions, reacts, and relates to the self and the phenomenal world.

There is a metaphor for the difference between the expression of the mind when it first arises, and for what happens when we then fail to use mindfulness and discernment. This metaphor is especially good for thinking about how mindfulness relates to Vajrayana practice and recognizing the nature of mind as we progress on the path.

Think about a stream. When at the place where the stream is bubbling right up out of the ground, the water from the spring is pure and clean and cold. But as we follow the stream farther and farther down the mountain, we see that it has had a long time to collect dirt, sediment, and decaying matter from the mountainside, and it becomes dirtier and dirtier. We can think about the experience of meditation as just like that. The first moment that any expression of energy arises from the mind is like that cold, clear, clean water. But as we get farther away from that moment, from its source, our discursiveness and conceptual thoughts get thicker and our emotions get stronger. The mental phenomena get "dirtier and dirtier," like the water that has been falling down the mountainside stream a long, long way. Mindfulness would have enabled us to recognize what was happening in the mind before that water made it to the bottom of the mountain. That is one way to understand the word "recognition" in the sense of recognizing the arisen conceptual thought the moment it first arises. If we can understand this metaphor, we will have some insight into how mindfulness and discernment are fundamental to experiencing the Dharmakaya.

Reflect on the quality of your life until now. According to the Buddhist teachings, karma has been accumulating since beginningless time and all of us have been accumulating all kinds of habitual tendencies. Even if we do not believe in past lives, just think about this one lifetime—all of the anger we have experienced, all of the sadness, the hatred, the greed, and the pride. Then think about the relative amount of time that we have spent training in meditation or positive aspiration or virtuous intent. This is only a comparative blink of an eye! So perhaps it's no wonder why the mind expresses the qualities that it does, and the kind of thick habitual tendencies we are working with as we train in mindfulness and discernment.

Extraordinary Mindfulness

As aspiring Vajrayana practitioners, the kind of mindfulness that we train in is not ordinary mindfulness; it is extraordinary mindfulness, the kind of mindfulness that allows us to recognize any expression of the mind the instant it is expressed—whether that expression be of afflictions, concepts, or clarity. Often when we talk about Dzogchen or Mahamudra practice, we talk about being able to recognize an afflictive emotion or conceptual thought and to transform it instantly. We are working toward training in *effortless* mindfulness, the kind of mindfulness that is as strong a habit as our ordinary discursiveness. When we train in ordinary mindfulness and discernment, we can think to ourselves, "I am taking a step in the direction of realizing the nature of mind. I am going to try to recognize what is going on in my mind as quickly as I can. One day I am going to recognize afflictive emotions the instant they arise." If we do that, we are moving in the right direction, toward authentic tantric practice. If we cannot recognize conceptual thoughts and afflictions the moment they arise, our practice does not reach the level of Dzogchen, no matter what we call it.

Contrary to what is often said among modern practitioners, it is extremely difficult to practice the kind of meditation that is called "self-liberation." This can basically be described as a "practice" where the moment an affliction or conceptual thought arises, the practitioner liberates it into the expression of meditation. This style of meditation cannot be conveyed in a book, it is experiential and must be transmitted by a genuine spiritual friend. But still we can have an idea that there is something profound to be understood and realized by describing it in words. Thus, we should generate a strong aspiration to do this if we are to succeed. We should say to ourselves, "I am going to master ordinary mindfulness and make it extraordinary."

However, we should be realistic about what we will see when we sit down to meditate. We should never have too high hopes such as, "Oh, my mind is really going to get clear really fast," or

"I am not going to have any more conceptual thoughts," or "I am going to stop having afflictive emotions or hatred toward the things that now make me upset." These are unrealistic expectations. It is also unrealistic to think that we are going to practice perfectly or that we are going to study perfectly; we are human beings and this makes us, by definition, fallible.

However, we know that we need to train in mindfulness and discernment, we know that there are techniques that are necessary not just for the practice of meditation, but also for the realization of the nature of mind. If we do not train in them, then our failure to become good practitioners is our own fault. The other things are not our fault, because we can only start where we are right now—here—today. But when we know what we need to practice and we do not, that is truly our own fault.

When students on the path study *Entering the Way of a Bodhisattva,* even though there is a whole chapter devoted to mindfulness and discernment, I still have the feeling that they do not realize the importance that this training has in our practice—especially for Vajrayana practice or meditation on the nature of mind. I also feel that this training is not emphasized as much as it should be by lamas and Vajrayana students alike in the West.

Take the example of going outside on a night when there is no moon and no stars; it is completely dark. You do not know which direction is north, south, east, or west. You do not know where to go. What if your feelings about meditation and the spiritual path were like that? What if you had no idea where to go? What would you do? How would you practice? How would you proceed? One of my goals in teaching on this topic is to give you a sense of feeling, "I know which direction I need to go in; I am certain about the kind of effort I need to make," so you do not waste your time and so you do not get discouraged or confused. It is hard to meet with Dharma and to have a genuine aspiration to practice. We should take every chance we have to cultivate our motivation and energy to practice.

Facing Suffering

We are Dharma practitioners, and even so, we are going to experience myriad sufferings in our lives. The Truth of Suffering is pinning us down in this very lifetime. We should remember that we are not going to find happiness right away just because we are Dharma practitioners. Our efforts at practice are not going to stop us from being accosted by suffering. What it really means to be a Dharma practitioner is that we must train in mindfulness and discernment so that we know how to use our practice when we experience suffering—in other words, we know how to help ourselves in the moments we encounter suffering. Being empowered to work through and transform difficulties and suffering is one of the most important goals of meditation.

It is very important that we become thoroughly convinced that there is no physical place where we can go to escape this suffering—escape all the things that we do not like, or escape the things that bother us. When I first came to America, many of the people I met were unhappy about the political situation here. One woman even told me she was planning to move to Canada to escape living under the then-current political administration. I found that ironic. I was actually very shocked to hear it. How could a Dharma practitioner believe that moving to another country would relieve her mind of its discontent? Didn't she realize that she would go somewhere else only to find new things that would make her equally unhappy? Didn't she realize that her ordinary mind was fundamentally conditioned to be dissatisfied? But the truth is, the first of the noble truths is really difficult to internalize.

It is equally important that we become convinced that the way to overcome or become flexible enough to accommodate everything in the world around us is through transforming the state of our own minds, not through ceaselessly trying to manipulate external conditions. This does not mean we become apathetic— we still work to make changes in our lives when necessary. However, we do so with a sense of balance, equanimity, and purpose rather than because of a motivation of anger or out of strong attachment. We should recognize that even if we had a life filled with every imaginable comfort and pleasure, suffering would still find its way in. There is simply no way to separate ourselves from suffering. Recognizing this, truly acknowledging it, is called the wisdom of no escape.

There are many types of suffering that we might experience in our lives. There might be small things that irritate us, there might be minor things that bother us, and there might also be very intense kinds of suffering. Some examples of intense suffering include natural catastrophes, fatal diseases, war, famine, or poverty. These are powerful, heart-wrenching experiences of suffering. A practitioner who has a thorough understanding and belief in karma, and who also practices meditation, will be able to work with even these situations with presence of mind. A true Dharma practitioner will be able to use even intense suffering as a condition to keep practicing and to generate compassion for the suffering of others. Lacking training in mindfulness and discernment, an ordinary person might not have the presence of mind to take such conditions to the path.

Maybe we are not experiencing intense suffering right now. In America as well as most Western countries, our lives are relatively good, speaking from a global perspective and in comparison to the kinds of conditions people have to face in the third world. But who knows the future? In our own lifetimes, we could be touched by war, terminal illness, or even famine. We will all encounter death. We should think to ourselves that when that time comes—because there absolutely will come a time that we are going to be overwhelmed by some kind of suffering—that our practice of meditation will be enough to help us through. That is why we practice. If we are not able to depend on our practice when times are the hardest, when we need it most, then what use has it been to practice?

When Tibetans leave the tent for the day, they always keep a piece of bread in their pocket. When they finally have a chance to rest by a cold stream, they sit down and eat their bread. It is always said in Tibet that if we practice meditation, and we do not use it when we need it, it is like starving and not realizing that we have a piece of bread in our pockets. In fact, it was useless to carry the bread in our pockets, for all the good it did us. This is just like forgetting to practice in the face of intense suffering—and how much more so in the face of comparatively minor suffering of, for instance, feeling anger at someone close to us.

If we forget to practice in that situation, it is equivalent to saying that we never really mastered mindfulness and discernment. We have the power to change our response in such situations. We have the power to alleviate our own suffering. But we must train ourselves to be able to call upon that power in our times of need.

Maybe a more pertinent analogy for the West is the situation of retirement. Imagine that we worked our whole lives and as we did, we saved money for retirement—as we are told is the wise thing to do. But, after retiring, we forgot that we had saved any money at all—and then we believed ourselves to be irremediably impoverished. We might believe we couldn't afford to buy food or afford to take care of ourselves. Obviously this scenario sounds absurd, doesn't it? But in our spiritual lives, this is exactly what happens all the time. We constantly miss opportunities to practice. We let them slip away and are controlled by the discursive mind, the mind that tells us stories of like and dislike. We forget what we can do in such moments. And again I come to this essential point: merging mindfulness and discernment with our daily lives will ensure that we do not forget to practice when it really counts—which is not when we are on our cushions, in a comfortable, air-conditioned room, sitting for a certain period of time.

I remember some advice my root lama gave me once before he died. He was imprisoned for a very long time after the Chinese came to Tibet. While he was imprisoned, the bone in his arm broke and was never reset. From that time on, he had trouble using it properly. My lama told me that a lot of people thought that they were yogis—even that they were great practitioners—but it was not until they went to prison that it was apparent who was a great practitioner and who was not, because until that time, life was easy enough that practitioners could be self-deceptive. It was not until they had to face such intense suffering that their meditation was tested through and through. My lama told me, "In the future, when hard times come, do not forget my teachings. If you forget at that time, then your whole life and your practice will have been wasted." For all the years since then, I have tried my best to abide by this instruction and not to waste my life.

That is also why it is said by members of the Kadampa lineage founded by the great teacher Atisha that whenever we have any kind of suffering of the five poisons, we should always let that be a condition for an even stronger positive motivation or more Dharma practice. The five poisons, of course, are the five root afflictive emotions: ignorance, anger, desire, jealousy, and arrogance.

We can also reflect on the story of Milarepa for inspiration on taking difficulties to the path. Without one of his uncles, he may never have gotten to the point where he became a serious Dharma practitioner. Milarepa's father died when he was young, and all of his family's wealth was hoarded by his uncle. When Milarepa grew old enough, he asked his uncle to return it. Not only did his uncle not give it back, he treated Milarepa and the members of his family like his servants. It was based on these experiences that Milarepa became filled with hatred, became a master of black magic, and killed many other beings. Then, one day, he finally experienced grave regret and met with the Dharma. Because Milarepa experienced hardship as a result of this relationship with his uncle, he was able to transform his life and his mind. He was able to train hard enough to become a buddha in one lifetime. This is a powerful example that teaches us that even amid suffering and the heaviest karma, we can still turn the situation around through diligent Dharma practice and achieve liberation.

There is another example that illustrates this same idea from the life of the great Nyingma master Longchenpa. When Longchenpa was still young, he became a great scholar. At that time, he was at a university in Lhasa, but he was surrounded by people from Kham. In Tibet, people from Kham are stereotyped as being very bad-tempered—jealous, argumentative, and possessive. When Longchenpa became a great scholar, the other scholars wanted him to become the head teacher of their university. All of the Khampas opposed it; they did not want Longchenpa to become a famous scholar. They resented him for being an outsider, for being different. They tried to block Longchenpa's rise to fame.

As a result of the conflicts that arose, Longchenpa gave up those aspirations for a prestigious life. He left Lhasa and wandered around Tibet, until he finally met his root lama Kumaradza. This was his karmic lama, who made him the holder of the Longchen Nyingthig lineage. After receiving the lineage teachings, Longchenpa stayed in retreat for the rest of his life and became a completely realized yogi. In his biography, Longchenpa talks about those times. He says something to the effect of, "When I was younger, I thought the Khampas were my enemies, but when I grew older, I realized that, without their kindness, I would never have become the person I became." He really expressed a lot of acceptance and even gratitude for those difficult and painful times that he had.

In the same way, many Tibetans' Dharma practice has, in a certain sense, actually benefited from the Chinese invasion. Many Tibetans have become better practitioners because of the hardship that they have undergone. They have become more compassionate, more outgoing, and more embracing of other people. Once again, we see that presence of mind can help us through the hardest of times!

No matter what kind of suffering we are experiencing, whether small or large, let us not be complacent. Let us all think about how we can bring that to the path and how we can increase our practice of meditation day by day.

Summary

Three ways to train in mindfulness moment by moment:

Reflect on the illusory nature of the three spheres.

Train in recognizing concepts and afflictions that arise in the mind at each moment. When the mind is agitated, remember to apply an antidote such as reflecting on the illusory nature of phenomena, or generating bodhichitta.

Cultivate the determination to use your Dharma practice when the mind is agitated. Each time you realize that you have missed an opportunity to practice because you have failed to recognize a disturbance in the mind, regret it and renew your aspiration and determination to recognize all future mental afflictions and conceptual thoughts.

CHAPTER 5

Mindfulness, Vajrayana, and the Spiritual Friend

It was said by the great master Shantideva that "Afflictive emotions should be examined by eyes of wisdom and abandoned." We could say that mindfulness and discernment give us eyes of wisdom. After all, what would wisdom or intellectual knowledge look like if it did not arise from mindfulness and discernment?

In a very loose sort of way, we can say it is possible for some kind of "wisdom" to arise from the afflicted mind, too. What is the difference between this and the primordially pure wisdom that is the true nature of all phenomena? This is something to examine through study and practice. It is definitely not a statement about which we should allow ourselves to remain confused.

In general, anything that arises from the mind has some kind of "wisdom quality" to it. Let us think carefully before we jump to conclusions about the meaning of this statement. I make this assertion from the point of view that, if the ordinary mind did not have some kind of quality of intellect or "wisdom" within it, the transformation of ordinary mind to wisdom would be impossible. In other words, that wisdom quality would first have to be present in the ordinary mind. It would also have to be present in anything that arises from the mind—even afflictions and conceptual thoughts—in order for transformation of afflic-tion to wisdom to be possible. If this were not the case, we would be creating wisdom from nothing at all, from no starting place.

Ultimately, it might be better to say that wisdom *arises* than that it is *created*. There is a big difference between these two state-ments. This is at the crux of my assertion that ordinary mind must have some wisdom quality.

Actually, any expression of the mind is—on some level—an expression of wisdom, but of course, it depends on how we are working with that expression. Again, we come back to the core idea that Dharma and Dharma practice completely depend on the individual.

This statement might lead us to think, "I do not have to rely upon mindfulness and discernment because any expression of the mind is already an expression of wisdom. So, even if that expres-sion seems very ordinary, it is actually wisdom. Can I not just abandon this whole course of meditation altogether?" It is true that I was just talking about the relationship between the ordinary mind and wisdom, and how what we perceive as an ordinary expression of the mind can be transformed into wisdom. But we should not jump to the conclusion that the potential for wisdom and wisdom itself are one and the same. If they were, we would not experience the sufferings of samsara. Since we all do experi-ence suffering, we should be clear that the mere potential for wis-dom to arise is not enough. The possibility of realization, in other words, is something precious—but it is not enough to carry us across the wide gulf between samsara and nirvana.

What is it that enables the ordinary mind to be transformed into wisdom? The short answer is—and of course must be—mindfulness and discernment.

Let us take the example of a great yogi like Milarepa to illustrate this point. It is probably easy for us to believe, based on what we know about Milarepa, that, in the later stages of his life, Milarepa unceasingly experienced the Dharmakaya. In other words, he recognized every expression that arose from his mind as the nature of mind itself. He saw each and every expression of mind as the play of wisdom.

But what about an ordinary practitioner who is not at the level of Milarepa? We also know that Milarepa was an ordinary and, we could also say, terrible practitioner at some points in his life. Somehow it was possible for Milarepa to transform his own mind. One of the reasons he went through many hardships was not only to develop diligence and to purify past wrongdoings, but also to have the chance to watch and intimately get to know his own mind. It was his chance to develop mindfulness and discernment.

Two Supporting Conditions

There are two supportive conditions that help us to train in mindfulness and discernment in order to further develop our meditation. The first condition is an outer condition. It is not something within the mind, but something that we have the ability to create around ourselves. The main part of this outer condition is working with an authentic spiritual friend or lama. Stories of the relationship between Milarepa and his lama, Marpa, are well-known by Buddhists far and wide because they exemplify how the spiritual friend acts as an outer condition for complete transformation. But I would also say that simply committing to a spiritual friend is not sufficient to make this outer condition

complete. Additionally, we need to have other committed practitioners around us, and we need to make an effort toward virtuous conduct and daily practice. By developing and maintaining
these connections, we will naturally begin to develop mindfulness
and discernment.

Based on a relationship with an authentic spiritual friend,
mindfulness and discernment arise naturally, because of the
exceptional nature of interdependent arising, the coming together
of causes and conditions that is the moment-by-moment expression of all phenomena. In Tibetan, we describe the nature of
interdependent arising to be something like the Western idea of
"positive energy." So developing a relationship with a lama is like
creating positive energy. This does not mean that our responsibility to practice has all been relieved. Additionally, I want to
qualify this statement by saying that it is not always the best thing
to rely upon a spiritual friend who always agrees with us or only
tells us what we want to hear. It is actually a lot more useful to
rely upon a teacher who will stand up to us and point out other
kinds of ideas—other ways of looking at things to help us get
outside of how we normally think. This helps us to break down
our self-attachment and extreme fixation on our habituated, comfortable way of thinking. I can remember little if any occasion on
which Marpa said anything to console or please Milarepa. Rather,
his fierce, selfless compassion enabled him to be the driving force
in Milarepa's glorious transformation.

There is a proverb in the Tibetan language that describes a
lama who is "white-hearted." What that means is a lama who
has a good aspiration for us, rather than one who is "black-
hearted" and wishes us harm—or perhaps is not really focusing
on our spiritual development but has some other motivation

mixed in with his or her teaching of the Dharma. Anyway, the proverb goes that the student often perceives the white-hearted lama as an enemy. The reason for this is that a lot of times when we are working closely with a spiritual friend, that spiritual friend is trying to cause us to give up some kind of attachment we have and fundamentally get us to open our minds. This is very painful to experience.

It can sometimes feel as if our teacher contradicts everything we say. If we say one thing, our teacher will say the opposite; then the very next day, he or she says what we said just the day before. This proverb was coined in Tibet because oftentimes we do not know how to deal with a white-hearted lama, despite the great kindness and service the teacher does us of revealing the contents of our minds.

Another reason why a spiritual friend behaves like this is that, based on the condition of contradicting us or doing something that we do not expect, he or she can create an opening or possibility for us to develop mindfulness, to discern what is happening in our own minds, and to reflect to ourselves, "What might be happening right now? What could I be learning from this?"

I remember once when my root lama wanted to give a profound transmission to another one of his students. However, when he just gave the words of the teaching, the student did not grasp its meaning. My lama waited a while, and then used a very unconventional method to teach him. One day when his student came in, my lama yelled at him and called him a thief. He had a fierce, angry energy. His student, who had great devotion, was shaken out of his normal state of mind. The moment opened up, and my lama was able to transmit the teaching to him. If his student had gotten angry, rather than entering into introspection about what his lama was trying to convey, he would have missed this incredible opportunity to learn!

Without the condition of the spiritual friend, we might never have the opportunity to examine our own minds. We often hear stories about yogis who lived many, many years with their masters. In some stories, the lama never gives any particular teachings—master and student just live together on a daily basis. For students who are truly devoted to their lama, this is a chance to learn the habits of mindfulness and discernment. Because the student is continually in the presence of her or his lama, he or she constantly has the chance to see him or herself though the lama's eyes. The student has a chance to escape from habitual ways of thinking and be totally open. Thus, in our tradition, simply by being in the presence of the lama and having to work with the way the lama interacts with them on a day-to-day basis, students undergo intensive mind training.

Since the Buddha Shakyamuni attained realization and began to convey the Dharma, it has been the standard for anyone who was a serious practitioner of meditation to live with a spiritual friend for at least fifteen years. This tradition was passed down directly from India to Tibet. I myself lived with my lama for fifteen years, and all of the great masters I know in Tibet have, at the very least, done the same. The reason was because, at that time, learning mindfulness and discernment was a high priority for practitioners. It was well known that training in mindfulness and discernment are the cause for meditative stability. The yogi would not usually consult the teacher about how to practice throughout his or her lifetime until after living for many years with the spiritual friend.

I can speak from my own experience, of course, because I was raised with a Dzogchen yogi, Lama Chupur, who lived with my family in our tent from the time that I was born. But also, later, I lived with my root lama, from whom I received all of my precious, secret oral instructions on the Longchen Nyingthig during the fifteen years I engaged in formal practice and study with him. Even after having lived with these two realized masters for so long, I am still not satisfied. I still do not feel like it was enough time. In my heart, I know I was not able to master all of the good qualities that my root lama had—especially his meditation and study habits, his mindfulness, and his discernment. For me, the longing to be close to my lama is like an unquenchable thirst.

Needless to say, the more time we can spend with an authentic spiritual friend, and whatever good fortune we have to receive words directly from that teacher, meant solely for us, the better it is. Honestly, I just do not feel I could ever be satisfied or get enough of my lama, no matter how many years I spent with him. We should do everything we possibly can to develop a personal, close relationship with a lama that we can spend time with regularly. Even though we cannot live like the yogis of old, we are fortunate that many great Buddhist masters either live in or visit the West regularly. With our own diligent effort, it is certainly possible to develop a close and personal relationship with an authentic master. After all, we are living in a country of abundant Dharma!

I have told stories to my students about Aku Tsembe before, usually about his cooking. Aku Tsembe was a yogi who stayed in retreat in the wilderness of an area of Tibet called Kham Minyak for many years. This was very near where my root lama lived. Anyway, the story I like to tell about him is how he would toss whatever he had into a pot and boil it up and call it soup. His soup was always full of strange and unique flavors—though that is perhaps a nice way of describing it. Once, when he gave me a bowl of soup, he asked me, "Isn't that delicious?" It was clear to me Aku Tsembe *did* think it was delicious—but truthfully, only a real yogi like him could think so. He was quite an extraordinary being.

What I wanted to tell you now about Aku Tsembe is how he only gave the same, single verse of Dharma instruction during his whole life. No matter what teaching I went to receive from him, he only gave this one teaching. I received it from him many times, though I asked for a full range of instructions from him—from foundational practices to the highest teachings of Dzogchen.

Aku Tsembe did not expound on a lot of teachings. All of his students were nuns and they lived in the same area practicing in various hermitages. But even though Aku Tsembe did not teach much through words, all the students of his that I ever met were really great practitioners—actually, they were truly amazing.

The verse that Aku Tsembe taught goes:

If there is attachment to this life, it is not Dharma
   practice.
If there is attachment to samsara, it is not renunciation.
If there is attachment to self, you are not a bodhisattva.
If there is any grasping at all, it is not the view.

Does this simple verse seem like a teaching that could encompass the wisdom of an entire lineage? When given in this way, in the context of this book, maybe not. But when Aku Tsembe gave the last two lines of the teaching, he would ask many questions of the people who came to see him. Doing so, he pointed out a great many things, from how to focus on the foundational teachings to how to abide in the nature of mind.

He was also fierce; he had a distinct kind of energy that is almost otherworldly. He shook you up so that the mind was humbled and open. It made the teaching quite different and much more profound than anything I can describe in a book.

Actually, if we went away thinking that this verse was Aku Tsembe's own teaching, we would be wrong. This verse was actually composed by a great Sakya master named Sakya Dragpa Gyaltsen. Sakya Dragpa Gyaltsen also meditated and taught on this verse his entire life; it was his main teaching. If we take some time really to reflect on these four lines, we will come to the conclusion that one who truly masters their meaning would indeed be a great practitioner of Dharma.

Even though I have just told you that this four-line teaching has the potential to help the mind to penetrate all other Dharma teachings, what is missing? Why do we hear the words of this verse and still not know how to put it into practice? That would be because our mindfulness and discernment are not at the level that enables us to practice this kind of teaching.

The outer condition of the spiritual friend tells us not only what to take up and, as a corollary, what to abandon; it also tells us what path to enter and what path not to enter. When we combine these instructions with the qualities of mindfulness and discernment, the quality of mindfulness enables us to remember the instructions; the quality of discernment enables us to know how and in what situations to apply them. When all of these conditions come together, the simplest of Dharma instructions become the cause for extraordinary realization. That is why pith instructions like these can be so simple as to be self-evident, yet at the same time can be penetratingly profound.

I also wanted to tell a story about another lama in Tibet named Khenpo Chukyap, who taught me something extremely important about mindfulness and discernment. This story illustrates how there is no condition like working with a lama to enable us to examine the mind.

Khenpo Chukyap was a yogi who had no possessions at all. I doubt that many have ever seen clothing as dirty as what this Khenpo wore. He probably had not bathed in years, if ever. Anyway, when I lived in Tibet, I was a very clean and neat person. I always took care of my appearance. One day, I went to see Khenpo Chukyap and when I knelt down in front of him, Khenpo Chukyap picked up a handful of ashes out of his hearth and threw them at me. At first, it was a little bit hard to bear. Honestly, it was quite shocking to have dirt and ashes flung upon me. But then Khenpo Chukyap said to me, "If your inner mind were as beautiful as you look on the outside, now *that* would be wonderful."

I thought about those words often. They really made an impression on me as a young monk. After that, whenever I went to see Khenpo Chukyap, I always wore ordinary clothes and was mindful about not putting too much energy into my outer appearance. He was pointing out a way for me to know myself better and to see how easy it is to be caught up in appearances.

My own root lama often scolded me and treated me in ways that were almost literally mind-blowing. He was a genuine, white-hearted lama in the very best sense of the term. Some of the lessons we are taught when we are close students of great masters are incomprehensible. But, even my root lama never did anything that shocked me as much as when Khenpo Chukyap threw the handful of ashes on me. I have never forgotten that.

While I cannot claim to have been able to totally embrace Khenpo Chukyap's filthiness either, I still know that I changed as a result of his profound, pith instruction.

The Inner Condition

Now that we have completed the discussion on the spiritual friend as the outer condition for training in mindfulness and discernment, let us turn to the inner condition. That condition is our own meditation. It is not what we generally think of as meditation—just stilling the mind—but meditation that is endowed with mindfulness and discernment. When we practice this kind of meditation, we are vigilantly remembering to engage in Dharma, and constantly reflecting on how to apply the instructions given by our lama. The thought continually arises, "Right now, should I be practicing in a certain way? If so, what should I be practicing?"

Practicing mindfulness and discernment properly has to do with balance. One extreme is making a huge effort that is completely exhausting. The other extreme is not making any effort at all.

Instead of doing either of these, we should always try to go right down the middle. The reason why falling into either extreme is harmful to practice is that neither extreme enables us to actually work with the mind. At one extreme, we are not working with mindfulness; we are not even thinking about it. We are completely lazy and unengaged. Because of that, we are not developing the skill to apply Dharma to real-life situations. In the other situation, we are trying to apply it to such an extreme that we lose focus on the mind altogether. That is why we need to go right down the middle.

Whether we think of ourselves as practitioners of sutra or tantra, it does not really matter. If we are skilled at working with mindfulness and discernment, people will look at us and think, "That is a skillful practitioner." And, unlike the other situations I have mentioned, they will be right! Being a skillful practitioner is not so much about where we are on the path; it has a lot more to do with what qualities we have in our minds and how those qualities support our meditation—wherever we are on the path. And ultimately it is the degree of mindfulness and discernment we have attained that causes us to progress more or less quickly.

Even if we go to see a lama who is teaching Dzogchen or Mahamudra and the lama gives us some kind of oral instruction to work with, it is really important to keep in mind that, without mindfulness and discernment, we will not be able to apply the teaching. We will not be able to use that teaching. I will talk more about merging mindfulness, discernment, and Dzogchen in the final chapter.

When we go before an authentic spiritual friend to receive teachings, that lama should be concerned with our level of mind training. Because they are teaching us out of the great aspiration of bodhichitta, spiritual friends should be concerned that in the future we remember and actually practice their teachings. Spiritual friends want us to develop good qualities as a result of meditation—that is the essence of teaching the Buddhist path.

But do not be fooled into thinking that we have no responsibility in the matter. It is not just up to the lama to have the positive aspiration for us. It is also up to us to ensure that we are able to practice the teachings. That is only possible because we are able actually to remember the teachings and the techniques the lama conveyed. Developing mindfulness and discernment will make us confident in this respect.

My root lama told me once that before he went to sleep each night, he would pray for each one of his students to become better practitioners and to realize the meaning of the teachings he had given them. As a humble student who does the utmost to emulate the great perfections expressed by my master, I continue this tradition of praying for the continued spiritual development and ultimate realization of my students and for each and every person with whom I have forged a connection. After reflecting on this, I hope that each of you, too, is making as much effort as you possibly can to practice. Please work on eradicating self-attachment, day and night!

Summary

Three ways to create inner and outer good conditions for realization by developing mindfulness:

Seek out and work at developing a relationship with an authentic spiritual friend.

Train in seeing the lama's every expression as a condition for mindfulness and discernment.

Engage in a consistent, daily practice to further develop natural and effortless mindfulness and discernment.

CHAPTER 6

Examining the Body-Mind Connection through Mindful Self-Reflection

Usually when we think about the word *Dharma,* we think about teachings that someone gives, or texts that explain the methods for different kinds of practice. But really, the true Dharma that we need to understand is that of the mind itself. We need to relate to our own minds. That is real Dharma.

Being in a position to practice Dharma at all, and then having the supreme good fortune to encounter it, is a very rare and precious thing.

It is very easy to become the mere reflection of a Dharma practitioner; but to become a Dharma practitioner who has all of the perfect conditions available to support his or her practice is a very difficult thing to do. We ought to reflect on the fact that we have at least some positive supports for Dharma practice. What good fortune we've had so far! But, the extent to which we use these supports to actually practice is really up to us. We also need faith and the will to practice.

Instead of having any spiritual inclination whatsoever, we might simply worry about making ourselves comfortable and happy. Or, we might focus on merely keeping our bodies healthy and looking young. In fact, in order to serve the body, we might actually push Dharma away.

It is important to examine the relationship between the body and the mind. For example, in this lifetime, the body and mind have an intimate connection. The idea of ego or the concept of self is created by each person's mind. The idea and experience of self-attachment are also created by the mind. From beginningless time, our minds have engaged in self-grasping. Even though our bodies have changed in form and appearance over time, we have always perceived ourselves in a fixed and lasting relationship with a particular body during a particular lifetime.

We can also reflect on the fact that what could be self-arisen wisdom has arisen as ordinary consciousness instead, because of the attachment that we have to the body. In other words, the attachment to the body keeps us from experiencing the nature of mind.

We must realize that the body can be used for either a worldly or a higher purpose. We can use the body itself as a support for meditation, so that it becomes a support for the practice of Dharma and enlightenment. But the body can also be the basis or support for accumulating negative karma, which will cause us to inhabit samsara continually.

When reflecting on the mind-body connection, one thing becomes apparent: we ordinary practitioners have not even realized the selflessness of our own self. We have not even realized that our ego does not exist, yet we want to go on and call ourselves practitioners of the Mahayana and the Vajrayana and use that to feel superior to and judgmental of others. Understanding the relationship between the mind and the body is a fundamental part of Dharma practice that enables us to see the basis of our self-attachment, so we should not neglect it. We should never give up an opportunity to cut through the ego's arrogance.

Just having a human life is not the same as having a precious human life. It is very important for us to contemplate and make choices about how we use our lives. It is important to treat this very lifetime as though it is precious. Simply realizing this life's impermanence is not enough to cut through self-attachment. Because few practitioners take up a life-long Dharma practice and delve deeply into a relationship with a spiritual friend to help them accomplish this, few can truly realize selflessness.

Self-Examination

We should take a moment to reflect on our Dharma practice from when we began practicing up until now. Have our afflictive emotions decreased since that time? Are we less angry, less dramatic, and less extreme? Are we less worried about the behavior of others and more mindful about our own behavior? Has our self-attachment decreased? Are we experiencing more clarity and stability in the mind? Are we able to practice more?

If, after making this examination, we feel that we are progressing pretty well, then it would be good to keep at Dharma practice just the way we have been. If we examine ourselves and then think, "I haven't changed as much as I should have as a result of practicing this long," it would be good to evaluate and reflect on ways that we could change.

Tibetan Buddhists say "the mind is not hidden from us"—in other words, we are the only one who can really see the qualities of the mind. It is the same idea we express in English when we say that no one knows us better than we know ourselves. We are with ourselves constantly, and only we have the ability to discern our true motivations. However, self-attachment and the ego are very seductive. It is very easy to be lured into thinking, based on our self-attachment, that "I'm doing really well. I'm a great practitioner." It is easy not to be objective in evaluating how our practice is going and what we are like as human beings. For example, it is difficult to reflect on situations as an outsider and consider how people perceive us. If we engaged in this mental exercise, we might start to have a different idea about who we are as compared to the person that we typically imagine ourselves to be.

In sum, whenever we engage in self-reflection, we must be objective. We must truly consider our progress and how we think our progress should be going.

If we find that we are not practicing with the same enthusiasm we had when we first began, we can use mindfulness and discernment to reflect on which habitual tendencies most often overpower us. There are a lot of possibilities. Perhaps we have a disposition that is really overpowered by laziness or distraction. We may also find that our faith degrades from time to time, and that this makes us lethargic. Sometimes our intellect might not be as sharp as usual. And, sometimes it is lack of diligence that afflicts us—we simply do not feel like making an effort at virtuous activity. It is normal to become overpowered by any of these tendencies from time to time, but we should become aware of our energy so that we know when we are overpowered. We should make an effort to correct it, so that we do not become even more overpowered. Then, we can shorten the period of time that the afflicted state lasts.

My root lama used to repeatedly quote a great master who said,

Even if you straighten a bent piece of wood
When it meets with moisture, it becomes crooked
    again.
Even if you reform the negative aspects of your
    personality
When you meet with the right conditions, you will
    show your faults.

Like that crooked piece of wood, it is natural for us to revert
back to how we were before—even though we may work very
hard at changing. It is so difficult for us to consistently apply the
mindfulness, discernment, and diligence that we need to keep
ourselves straight. I reflect on this all the time; I think that it is one
of the most important teachings that my lama ever gave me. He
said it so many times about me in front of huge audiences of people, which was difficult to bear—it was extremely embarrassing.
But now I find this particular piece of advice very valuable.

The Seduction of Practice

One of the ego's greatest seductions is tricking us into believing
that we have attained realization or some unusual sign as a result
of our meditation. In these circumstances, we should notice what
is happening in the body, but never get attached to it. We should
strive to never generate hope or craving toward any particular
meditative state. This is one of the most important ways in which
we can apply mindfulness and discernment.

A great yogi named Drupa Konlok said that when some people start to practice meditation, they have a physical experience in
the body, which we often refer to as heat or bliss. Drupa Konlok

said that it was very easy for a beginning practitioner to mistake this for the primordially pure view, or think that somehow this ordinary state is the profound experience of clarity and emptiness. He urged us not to make this mistake, and I also urge you to be careful. We must be very objective about our own practice. We should not be seduced by thinking that we are experiencing something profound, when that experience does not match what is described in the teachings as a profound state. We should not be tricked into wanting something so badly from our meditation that we fabricate experiences.

It is also said that when a practitioner experiences the heat of bliss in the body as a result of practice, the most dangerous thing the practitioner could do is to have any kind of attachment or desire to abide in that state, or to experience it again. If we persist in hoping to experience that state, the scriptures state that we will be reborn into the samsaric suffering of the form realm. When we analyze our own practice, we should not be seduced by ego. For all of these reasons, we must learn to be objective about our experiences!

When we are objective about our experiences, we are free of hope and fear. We do not wish to use them as ego-support. Often times, we want to use our experience as evidence to show that we are special, unique, skillful, or wise. When we are objective, we witness our experiences neutrally and continue to practice.

Abide in the Experience of "No Self"

From the point of view of the Theravada Buddhist teachings, there are many methods laid out for realizing the selflessness of the self as opposed to selflessness of phenomena. It could be said that the Theravada tradition teaches that the self of an individual is empty, but does not provide methods for realizing the emptiness of outer phenomena. Thus, realization based on these teachings is profound, but not complete.

If a practitioner realizes the selflessness of the self, based on the Theravada teachings, it is of course still possible later to take up the practices of the Mahayana and the Vajrayana in order to finally attain a state of complete realization.

However, one practice that every practitioner can engage in is examining the body and trying to find out if there is anything permanently abiding within it. In other words, is there some inherent existence in the body?

The first thing that will happen when we examine this is that we may think that there is no real self. I say this from the point of view of intellectual experience. For, if we simply apply the Buddhist teachings on impermanence and emptiness, a cursory analysis shows that the self is simply a concept. There is no lasting, permanent self that abides beyond or escapes death. While this is somewhat helpful for developing a Buddhist foundation, ultimately, it will not take our practice to the next level. This is because ordinary practice does not give us a profound way to cut through the mind's grasping. Merely knowing is not the same as experiencing and realizing.

Instead, if we were able to abide in that experience of "no self," we would find that our examination of the body and the true experience of meditation can be brought together, synthesized. A practitioner who has experience in Dzogchen practice, or who knows how to abide in clarity and emptiness, can use his or her practice at that moment. No matter how experienced we are, actually sitting down from time to time and reflecting on whether the self inherently exists is still an important practice. In the beginning, this technique seems limited, but when we apply our own skills in working with the nature of mind to the technique, it is actually unlimited.

There was some good advice given in a teaching by a profound scholar named Mipham Rinpoche called *The Wheel of Meditation and Examination*. The advice was for beginning practitioners, but I think it is useful to practitioners of all levels when we apply it to Vajrayana meditation. The advice is basically to let the mind grasp at whatever concept happens to arise in it consistently, until we become tired of grasping at it.

Because we have been training diligently in mindfulness and discernment, we begin to notice the repetition of the mind's continual obsession. This causes us to start to develop a real sense of distaste for it. Our distaste enables us to slowly form the resolve to change. Once we have resolved to change, each time we notice the mind grasping at the same old situation, we strengthen our resolve. Finally, we become attuned enough to the mind's habit that we get tired of this repeated grasping and we are able to cut through it.

For example, when we practice, we might get distracted over and over again by the sound of the television or a phone conversation that is happening in some other part of the house. If we simply allow ourselves to get annoyed and irritated by this over and over again, one day we will simply get tired of letting this small thing interrupt our peace of mind. I once met a practitioner who said that when he first began to meditate, he asked his wife and children to be perfectly quiet so as not to disturb him. He got angry if they made any noise whatsoever while he was practicing. Later he realized that this was actually the opposite of meditation. Meditation is about making the mind spacious enough to accept and let everything in. It is not about controlling the environment so as to shut everything out.

When the mind gets tired of grasping, we are able to abide in a deeper experience of meditation. By using this instruction each time we notice a strong habitual tendency in the mind, eventually we will be able to abide in clarity and emptiness through this instruction—combined with the proper oral instructions and transmissions from our spiritual friend. Again, we see how any simple technique can give rise to something profound.

The Qualities of Lama and Student

The great master Milarepa said,

> It is difficult to meet a compassionate lama endowed with
> Transmissions, textual mastery, and oral instructions.

We may have many of the conditions necessary to support our Dharma practice, but one of the conditions that Milarepa specifically pointed out when he gave this teaching was the importance of connecting with a spiritual friend. We have already talked some about the importance of a spiritual friend, but here Milarepa reminds us that not just any spiritual friend will do. Our spiritual friend must have had the proper transmissions, the proper kind of intelligence, the proper kind of oral instructions or practice lineage, and also the proper kind of bodhichitta. Specifically, the transmissions and oral instructions must be of a pure, unbroken lineage of teachings such as the Longchen Nyingthig. The spiritual friend's intelligence must be such that he or she can present teachings in a way that make sense to and can benefit a variety of students. And, the spiritual friend's bodhichitta must be untarnished by any self-interest or selfish motivation. Milarepa also said,

> Even if you practice sacred Dharma,
> It is difficult for all the perfectly pure conditions to
>   come together.

It is a good idea to reflect on whether we feel that we have all of the conditions that we need to support our Dharma practice. If we do not have the conditions that we need, it is good to think about how we might take steps to invite or create these conditions around us. This is a highly personal kind of self-reflection. For example, if you feel you need a regular place to sit where other people are gathering to practice, do your best to seek out that kind of situation for yourself.

Not only is an authentic spiritual friend hard to meet and connect with, it is also hard for a student to have all the proper qualities to be an excellent practitioner. Returning again to Milarepa:

> It is difficult to meet a student with the potential to
>   practice
> Who is not disheartened; whose faith and endurance
>   do not become exhausted.

Some of the qualities that Milarepa named as being important in a student were having devotion—not only to the spiritual friend, but also to the teachings—having the proper kind of respect, having mindfulness and discernment, and being able to make consistent effort. Another really important quality we can cultivate is the resolution not to be easily disappointed, disheartened, or disillusioned with Dharma practice. This happens to everyone from time to time. We are all human beings with the capacity to experience disappointment. But if we allow our disappointment in the unsatisfactory nature of samsara to overwhelm us, we will lose our enthusiasm for practice. It is our own responsibility to ensure that we do not lose our motivation and enthusiasm to practice.

Let us all think about the kind of hardship that we could undertake for our practice of Dharma. How much suffering—how much could we really bear in order to increase our practice? I think the realistic answer to this question is humbling. Often, the answer we come up with is, "not very much at all." This mental exercise should show us something about our own character and our own faith.

When we reflect on this idea, we do not even have to compare ourselves to the really great practitioners like Longchenpa or Milarepa. Milarepa is a yogi famous for enduring extreme hardship to receive teachings from the great scholar Marpa. In fact, he was told to build and tear down nine towers before Marpa would teach him. Each time Marpa denied his request, Milarepa was overwhelmed with disappointment and despair, but he never gave in. Out of his yearning for the Dharma and his devotion to his lama, he endured this hardship until Marpa finally agreed to teach him. Milarepa, who had already developed heroic diligence, attained enlightenment in a single lifetime as a result.

Likewise, the great master Longchenpa endured the extreme hardship of staying in retreat for seven years with only a bag woven of yak wool for bedding and clothing, and very little food, as he practiced the teachings given by his root lama Kumaradza. He is another example of a master who was able to attain enlightenment in a single lifetime as a result of his heroic effort and forbearance.

Even in our dreams, it would be hard for us to imagine going through the kind of hardship that they went through for Dharma. We must think about our ordinary lives and some of the things that we can do to increase our energy and effort toward Dharma. Some of the things that are in our grasp are simply committing to daily practice—or increasing the practice that we already do— and training in bodhichitta whenever we meet with the appearance of our own or others' suffering.

We should all feel encouraged because we do have some ability and capacity to practice the Dharma, even if it is not like that of some of the great masters. We have to remember that it is up to us to be motivated and to actually engage in practice. This is not something that another person can do for us, although someone's example and support might help us do it ourselves. We will not change without the effort of our own will.

Yet I can say with certainty that there is not one person that does not have the ability to have a consistent practice of meditation on a daily basis. Every person is capable of doing that. Every person can do it without missing any days if they dare to make a serious commitment. Having this kind of commitment to daily practice is one of the main supports for Dharma as a whole.

If we ever feel like we are too busy to practice Dharma, we can take a moment to reflect on all the things that we do that we feel we do have time for. Almost everybody has time to, for instance, watch a program on TV. People want to do things that make them feel like they have no responsibility. They want to relax and feel like they do not have to think about anything. Even if we took only a little of that time that we devote to other things, we would be capable of having a consistent daily practice.

That is why the great master Milarepa said,

> It is difficult to take up meditation for your whole life
> Even if all the other conditions come together.

It is very difficult to make the time to practice on a consistent basis. We may find that simply making the time and the commitment to practice is the hardest part of becoming a genuine practitioner.

One way we can work on developing a habit to practice is by considering for how long we could consistently commit to practice each day. It may only be five or ten minutes when we begin. We should take this as the minimum for our daily practice. Then, we should commit to completing at least this much practice every day for one hundred days. No matter what happens, we should resolve not to give up. At the end of the hundred days, we can reevaluate the length of practice time we have chosen. We may want to increase it, or simply keep it the same, before we make another time commitment for practice. If we work with short periods of commitment that are not too overwhelming, over time we will find that we have developed the habit of daily practice without falling into any self-defeating behavior.

Life Is Fleeting

The body is like a fragile bubble. As time passes, it breaks down and becomes weaker and weaker. In light of this, we should use the body as a support for practice, and practice as much as we can from this moment forward.

Even when we are young and strong and our bodies can withstand a lot, we are so attached to our bodies that we put them ahead of everything else. For example, if we are practicing prostrations, we might notice that after about a hundred prostrations, or maybe even fewer, somewhere in the body a sharp pain comes and we do not want to do prostrations any more. It could be the knee, or the hand or the stomach. This is the intersection between the body as a support for practice and as an obstacle to practice. I do not suggest that we physically hurt ourselves doing prostrations but I do suggest we reflect upon how much power we give to our physical experiences.

One of the reasons I bring this up has to do with my root lama. When my root lama was eighty-five years old, he was still doing three thousand prostrations every day. Not only that, but as I mentioned previously, his arm had been broken and was never correctly set when he was younger. The bone never healed properly, so one of his arms would just hang at his side. He could not use it well. He was doing prostrations basically using the strength of only one arm. When you reflect on this, doesn't it seem like the ability to engage in that kind of intense, physical practice has to do with our self-attachment? It has to do with the level of importance we place on the physical experience of pain, and our level of mind stability. Profound mind stability enables great masters to do things that ordinary people feel are impossible. And this can enable us to work with the energy of pain in a different way so that we can continue practicing.

This story is meant to be illustrative of how the mind is more powerful than the body and how our experience in the mind transforms the way we experience everything. I will not be dishonest with you; if I had to prostrate three thousand times every day, it would be very difficult. It was really quite miraculous that my root lama could do that.

One thing that happens as a result of living in such a developed country as this is that we can be a little bit lazy about our bodies in terms of ordinary things. The great Kadampa masters in Tibet all lived in caves. They had no mats, no sofas, and no pillows. They were able to live in nature, make do with simple shelters, and bear the conditions that were there.

Our lives in the West are full of wonderful comforts. We have sofas, beautiful rooms for sitting, and cool places to rest. Sometimes, this can make us lazy. We might think, "I am so comfortable here relaxing, I don't really want to get up and practice Dharma." On one hand, we can use these comforts in a positive way; on the other hand, they can become distractions. This is just another way of saying that it would be better for the mind to dictate what we do, and to transform everything in our environment into support for our Dharma practice.

I do not advocate asceticism. I know that there are some religions where it is supposedly good to cut yourself or do something harmful to your body in the name of purifying it. Buddhism does not suggest we do this at all. My words are meant to cause everyone to think about how dominating the desire for physical comfort is, and how much this, in turn, dominates our energy and time.

Reflect on Impermanence

Something that we should constantly reflect on is the impermanence of life, of our own and of others', especially those we love. We should not only be mindfully grateful that we are physically healthy, but also that we do not have too much mental suffering—however dark our minds may feel, right now at least we are able to reflect on the Dharma. It is most important for us to create a strong foundation in Dharma practice when we are healthy and not too overpowered by suffering. If we wait until we are sick or dying or very old or until we are experiencing some kind of intense suffering, we would find that it is much harder to practice at that time. So the best time to practice is always now.

Many years ago, my great uncle passed away; he died of cancer. He was a lifelong practitioner and his lama was also my root lama's teacher. Needless to say, my great uncle was quite old when he died. He had received special Dzogchen transmissions, and he was a serious practitioner of those teachings. Actually, most people never realized what a good practitioner he was until he passed away, especially me. Yet as he neared his death, the strength of his practice became clear. Before his death, he should have been in great pain because of his cancer. But his *mind* was peaceful. In fact, I think it was harder for us to watch him than it was for him to experience the cancer himself. Just before he died, an old lama came to see him and read him some teachings. Then, just before his breathing stopped, my uncle asked the lama, "Is it all right now?"—asking if the lama thought that my uncle had done all that could be done to prepare. The lama agreed, and my uncle died serenely. There were two remarkable things about his death. The first was that he genuinely did not seem to experience suffering as he died from cancer. The second remarkable thing became clear when, according to Tibetan custom, we kept the corpse isolated for two weeks. During this time the corpse shrank to a very small size—which is one of the signs of realization of the Dzogchen teachings. They cremated the body on a stormy day—and I can attest to more auspicious signs, hard as that may be to believe: not only did rainbows appear, but the bones became rainbow-colored after they were burned!

Keep in mind that lifelong practitioners who train seriously in mindfulness and discernment have the potential to rest in the nature of mind at the time of death. The lives and deaths of many great masters, as well as the scriptures, attest to the fact that death provides a unique opportunity for us to attain complete liberation if we are able to practice as we are dying, or after we have died. If we are such practitioners, we will be able to recall our lama's instructions on our deathbed and die in our lama's presence, actualizing his or her instructions and carrying them out. That will transform the experience of death. This is something to prepare for very seriously.

But to be able to practice mindfulness at the moment of death, we need to practice vigorously now. We could have the attitude of procrastination. We could reflect and say, "This year I am so busy. I am going to become a real, committed practitioner next year," or "I am going to retire in ten years so I will become a practitioner then." Please reflect on the fact that each time we inhale, we have no idea if we will be alive to exhale. Every time we inhale and exhale our lives become shorter. Life only exhausts itself and death is our shadow. We have no idea how long we will be able to live or if and when we will have the chance to do anything at all. The attitude of procrastination is completely incompatible with any goals or inclinations that we could possibly have for Dharma practice.

The younger we are when we start to practice, the easier it will be to attain results of that practice. This does not mean that it is impossible to practice as we get older; it just means that the actual physiology of the body and brain—for example, the sense faculties and the channels, energy, and essences—all begin to degrade as the body becomes older. So, the younger we are when we begin to make an effort at practice, the easier it will be for us. We could liken it to a physical practice like yoga, where it is obviously easier for a person who is younger to master some of the asanas, the poses. This does not mean that it is impossible when we are older—after all, nothing is impossible. So even if you are old now, do not despair. Starting to practice mindfulness and discernment now will surely be a boon. But please do not waste another moment.

A metaphor in the sutras says that sometimes the sky is clear and at other times it is cloud-covered. No one knows when the clouds will cover the sky. One of the meanings of this saying is that we have no understanding of when birth and death will come. It is just like watching a movie; the story of our life and death has a life of its own, wholly beyond our control and our will. Since I left Tibet, all of the old monks in my monastery have died. At least thirty monks I have known have died just in the past few years—that amazes me. Simply realizing that old practitioners are dying motivates me to practice.

One thing that happens in the West is that it is much harder for us to even notice old age and death in our society. In the West, people do not often live with their parents like Tibetans, watching our parents grow old day by day as we live with and care for them. In the West, not only do we not witness this, but sometimes we tend to avoid it, pushing it away out of sight and of mind—

we do not talk about it. We do not go places where we might have to look at it.

In poor countries, people have to coexist with birth, old age, and death all the time because there is no alternative, no way they can turn away and pretend to escape it. In my experience, this is one of the reasons why people in undeveloped countries have a lot of motivation to practice Dharma. They are always staring death in the face. They are always reflecting on when they will die, and what death will be like. And that can be great Dharmic inspiration!

Please think about death and impermanence. When I do that, I just want to practice. I want to build more Dharma foundation for my death. Please don't live in a way that you end up with a lot of regrets at the moment of death.

Summary

Five techniques for working with mindfulness and the body:

Analyze the body's impermanent nature. Attempt to take this beyond a merely intellectual experience, abiding in the experience of "no self" if possible.

Let the mind get tired.

Take a mental inventory of what you need to commit to practice, and work to surround yourself with those conditions. Especially, work on developing a close and personal relationship with a lama as much as possible.

When you notice the body overpowering the mind, reflect on the body's impermanence and bring the mind back into balance.

Reflect on the fleeting quality of life. Cultivate enthusiasm and motivation to practice every day.

CHAPTER 7

Working with Wind Energy to Perfect the Mind

It was said in a vajra song composed by Nyagla Padma Dudul:

The karmic wind is a prancing, flying wild horse
Ridden by the childish mind.
[When] the demons of immediate conceptual
    thoughts stir [the mind] up
It runs into the plain of habituated laziness.
Pull on the bridle of mindfulness!

In the previous chapter, we began to explore the body-mind connection. In this chapter, we're going to do that in a slightly different way. Now, we are going to focus more on the movement of energy in the body and how that affects the mind, and also how this can benefit or harm the practice of meditation.

To begin a discussion of this topic, I want to raise the idea of a connection between wind energy—which we can in some cases call the breath—and what the mind expresses. Wind energy is obviously a physical, bodily component. Before we begin cultivating mindfulness, it is probably an aspect of the body that we are not used to noticing. Or, because of its close connection with the mind, we may not have realized that our wind energy is an aspect of the body at all. The rush of energy might just seem like a normal, emotional response whose physicality is a mere side effect.

To understand the importance of working with wind energy, and to see the connection between wind energy and mindfulness, let us first contrast meditation based on the sutras to that based on tantra. When practicing meditation according to the sutras, we try to recognize whatever afflictive emotion is present, or whatever is happening in the mind. In short, our practice is one of noticing and also of trying to apply an antidote. We try to abandon whatever afflictions we recognize so that they do not cause us mental and emotional suffering. We have been talking about this process in the context of ordinary mindfulness and discernment thus far.

Let us review what this looks like during our actual sitting practice, when we are trying to meditate. We begin with an awareness of the mind's relative clarity or wildness. The very first instant that some kind of affliction, thought, feeling, memory, or concept arises in the mind, we try to recognize it and apply an antidote—whether it is simply abstaining from grasping at the concept or feeling, developing bodhichitta, or reflecting on impermanence. Then, we begin our meditation again.

When we think about it this way, we can see how difficult it is to apply the oft-spoken idea from the Vajrayana teachings that we are simply supposed to somehow instantaneously recognize and experience an affliction as being wisdom. This is something that we are ill-equipped to do unless we specifically train in a style of meditation that makes this possible. Instead, the way that we usually work with an afflictive emotion is to notice that it has arisen and then, in hindsight, try to apply some kind of antidote.

When we apply an antidote, it is like running to get buckets of water to pour onto a fire that is burning up a grassy meadow. By the time we try to douse the flames, the fire is already raging out of control. If we reflect on that metaphor, it shows us the lapse between when the affliction arises and the point at which we can work with it. In short, we cannot—are simply not capable of—working directly with the afflictions that cause us suffering when we take up meditation based solely on sutra study.

Through the kindness of the spiritual friend and the profound pith instructions of Dzogchen and Mahamudra, as well as our gradual mastery of mindfulness and discernment, we learn how to put out the wildfire when it is just a spark. It is important to realize that this is something entirely different than what we have been talking about up until now.

In other words, for ordinary practitioners, there is no direct connection being made between the practice of meditation and the mind's continually arising afflictions. Because the mind does not recognize afflictions as they arise, we always find ourselves in a state of chasing after the mind's distractions. We are always doing something in hindsight, trying to improve something that has gone bad. When considering this idea, it makes sense that the scriptures say that sutra practitioners must work to perfect their practice over a very long period of time. The length of this time cannot even be quantified, and indeed it is described as countless lifetimes.

To understand the importance of mastering tantric practice, reflect on this: we can never actively change the energy of the mind on the spot if we are always looking back and thinking, "How can I change that? What can I do to revise my action or purify whatever just happened?" We have already accumulated the action's negative karma. We now have even more karma to purify through practice. Of course, karma can be purified—that is one benefit of practicing meditation. But a great master who understands how to self-liberate the mind's afflictions through the use of tantric instructions arrests the process of accumulating karma, and proceeds to purify the stock of karma already accumulated, both in the same moment.

Using Mindfulness and Discernment to Balance Our Energy

We have talked about the fact that we are not directly working with the afflicted mind when we work with meditation according to the sutra teachings. I want to clarify that my words do not mean that these teachings have no benefit, rather the result is less potent or needs a longer time to take effect.

In comparison to what I have just described, tantric meditation is basically a revolutionary approach. Tantric meditation requires uncommon training, intelligence, faith, and perseverance as well as an uncommon connection with an authentic spiritual friend—but the sum of these creates the opportunity to relax into the mind's own intrinsic nature; its vast spacious quality. But just how does this happen? The answer to this question is simple if we properly understand the teachings on mindfulness and discernment.

To tie the teachings on mindfulness and discernment to Vajrayana practice, I would like to revisit the idea that there is a very strong relationship between the mind and wind energy. A practitioner who has mastered working with wind energy or breath has also mastered the method to purify and dispel obstacles.

Wind energy is subtle and difficult to notice at first. To understand the meaning of this teaching, we can try to notice this personally, in our own bodies during our own meditation practice. It might not be readily apparent in the beginning. Whether we are sitting or just going about our daily lives, whenever we notice that we are having a lot of conceptual thoughts—this is created by the rising of wind energy up through the body. When we feel agitated, that the mind is afflicted, or that we are suddenly emotional, that is also the result of rising wind energy. When we are sitting down and suddenly feel like we have to get up and go do something else—that too is the result of agitated wind energy. The impulsive nature that dominates the West especially demonstrates that people in this culture have a tendency for high wind energy, more so than people in Asia. This is probably both a cultural and physiological trait of westerners.

In Tibet, we use the metaphor of boiling milk to illustrate how too much wind energy creates instability. If the fire is too hot in the beginning, the milk boils over and bubbles spill all over the place—and the milk loses its energy. We need to learn to balance our energy as practitioners. If we allow too much energy to build or surge up at one time, we cannot sustain the energy to practice. We need mindfulness and discernment to catch when our energy becomes erratic. That way, we can train in having more consistent energy in both the body and the mind.

If we cannot learn to handle our impulsiveness, we will fail to retain anything and be like the mere appearance of practitioners whose insides are hollow vessels. Instead, while we have these good conditions to support personal transformation, we need to learn to restrain or harness our energy so that we can apply it in a consistent way. We should avoid the fault of forgetting to practice what we have learned.

One support for developing this quality of remembrance is

daily practice. Whatever we are practicing, if we are working on bodhichitta, a daily practice, or ngondro practice, it is important that we do not practice sporadically. We should practice consistently. The lama may not ask us whether or not we are practicing, but he or she can certainly tell. It is like seeing smoke billowing up into the sky—we know a fire must be burning down below. Or, when we see water birds flying, we know there must be a lake beneath them. People do not have to be psychic to know what we are doing or what is happening in our minds. It is actually not that hard to see what is happening in someone's mind. We are not as good at keeping secrets as we may think.

Perhaps it is not an optimistic thing to say, but I feel that in the modern age there are not many masters who have maintained all of the techniques of working with wind energy. But, there are still a few pure lineages that exist, such as the lineage of my own lama, Dorlo Rinpoche. He was one of the greatest modern masters of wind energy in Tibet. He was a master at working with all kinds of energy, including practices like *tummo,* or generating heat. If we lack faith that training in wind energy can be truly miraculous, simply meeting a master like this can quickly change our minds.

When we feel that our practice is successful—that it is actually benefiting us the way it is meant to—it is because we have noticed the relationship between our wind energy and our meditation, and have had some insight on how to work with that relationship. This will happen when we start working with a lama, and that lama gives us some pointers or techniques that enable us to gain some experience in working with wind energy. Needless to say, any practitioner who wants to gain stability in the practice of meditation is going to need to gain a lot of experience in working with that energy. And, I probably do not need to point out again the essentiality of a spiritual friend.

Karmic Breath, Wisdom Breath

In general, the teachings on wind energy focus on two different kinds of wind energy. Perhaps here it is easier to use the word "breath," because we usually associate this type of wind energy with exhalation and inhalation. The other kinds of wind energy do not resemble the breath, but rather energize and create movement in other bodily systems, such as digestion or circulation. However, these two types of wind energy that I am going to introduce now are often referred to as karmic breath and wisdom breath. The difference between these two is that karmic breath is breath that agitates us, while wisdom breath enables the mind to abide in a profoundly vast and relaxed state.

To recognize the experience of the karmic breath, we should begin by noticing what the body—especially the abdomen and chest—feels like when the mind is agitated. When our wind energy is high, we will feel physically agitated. Sometimes we feel hot, impulsive, or erratic. We will notice that the more agitated the mind is, the less control we have over our discursiveness.

On the other hand, if we are able to release the karmic breath, which is a technique given in *tsa lung* or teachings on channels, energies, and essences, we will notice that this has the effect of dispelling those myriad thoughts and afflictions in the mind. An authentic spiritual friend can give instructions in some of the simpler methods for doing this, instructions that are suitable for any level of practitioner.

Although all we can do in the beginning is try to recognize the karmic breath, I will give one simple technique that can enable us to dispel it after we learn how to use the technique properly. Before we begin sitting practice each morning, we can slowly and mindfully exhale and inhale in a series of three or nine times. Each time we exhale, we can follow the breath until it naturally dissolves. Generally, there is a gap where no breath is necessary. If we know how, we can rest in the view of clarity and emptiness there. Then, we inhale again and follow the breath down into the abdomen. Again, there is a gap before we exhale where we can rest if we know how. If we make too much effort as we breathe, the breath becomes more difficult to control.

After the final exhalation, we inhale and swallow the breath down with our saliva and, ideally, hold it near the navel. This last instruction seems cryptic, and the meaning is not easily discernable. However, after much repetition it begins to make sense experientially. This instruction should be followed regularly, but not more than once a day.

Although I have given this simple instruction on paper, I always advocate receiving such instructions directly from a lama, so that the student has a chance to ask questions and clarify the meaning.

The other kind of wind energy I am going to introduce at this point is called wisdom breath. This is a very subtle, almost imperceptible breath that happens when we are resting in the nature of mind. The only time that we are able to notice and experience wisdom breath is when our karmic breath has been released. With even a little bit of experience in working with the karmic breath and the wisdom breath, we will start to gain the necessary foundation for working directly with afflictive emotions, rather than just applying something in hindsight. That is when we will be able to engage in tantric practice. I do not mean to say that this alone will transform our practice, but it will certainly make the practice of Dzogchen a possibility. In other words, this is one basis for transforming concepts directly into wisdom.

So, let us examine the relationship between mindfulness, discernment, and the karmic breath. If we consider, in hindsight, the experience of energy in the abdominal area and chest—especially when we are agitated or upset—we will quickly get to know karmic breath. However, without mindfulness and discernment, we cannot notice our wind energy and the subtle way it rises through the body until it is pronounced and strong. At this point, we are already overpowered by some kind of affliction. We are not going to realize that we need to practice; we are not going to realize that karmic breath is a source of our agitation. This is like the fire we mentioned earlier—the one that is burning out of control before we even notice that it started.

We can think about the relationship between the wisdom breath and the karmic breath as being like a scale or balance. However strong the karmic breath becomes, the wisdom breath becomes correspondingly weak and weighed down, and vice versa.

It is important to master the wind energy because, at some point, the ability to work with wind energy and the ability to abide in the nature of mind become one and the same experience. Yogis who are able to work with this singular experience have diligently trained in recognizing the karmic breath when it comes up, and also know the way to release it. I am not talking about this release happening in hindsight as in the discussion of sutra practice. The recognition and release are happening simultaneously. Going back to our metaphor, we are snuffing the spark in the first instant before the fire has the chance to catch.

Holistic Practice

When I teach, I almost always try to present a teaching from the point of view of the sutra and then the same teaching from the point of view of the tantra, to show how the two are complimentary and work together. In this case, if we are able to see the value in developing the fundamental skills of working with the mind, such as mindfulness and discernment, it is logical that we will become better practitioners. I also believe that when we take up techniques from both the sutra and the tantra, our understanding is more comprehensive and therefore we find it easier to obtain a result.

In order to truly understand the kind of skills we need to develop here and now on the path, each of us should consider the kind of practitioner we want to become in the future. This can be an important source of motivation.

I do not mean to confuse anyone by contradicting one of the well-established tenets of Buddhism, "The path is the goal." This phrase describes how just practicing, with no attachment to outcomes, is the ultimate aspiration of any practitioner. However, in the beginning I do think we have to be a bit more pragmatic. Without focusing our attention on the example of a being who has greater capacity than we each have currently, it is hard to develop any faith or energy toward the path at all. The difference comes down to the way we work with the example we choose. What I am advocating is not so much setting a goal as looking toward a beacon, something that can guide us on a long, turbulent ride. After all, if we want to practice as a bodhisattva, we absolutely need to be committed to cutting through our self-attachment and increasing our wisdom for the long haul.

To illustrate the point, consider a highly realized being—yet one who is only in the first stage of realization. This being would have realization equivalent to the realization of Nagarjuna. Even this first stage of realization is far beyond us ordinary beings. Such realization follows a direct experience of the nature of emptiness, yet this is only the first stage of realization. Because the bodhisattva has experienced emptiness directly, all afflictive emotions have been cut through.

Looking at that bodhisattva's mind from our own point of view, though, we could say that the experience would be the same as the instantaneous liberation of an affliction or conceptual thought. Another way of saying this is that at the very same moment the energy of delusion arises, wisdom naturally and simultaneously expresses itself. This is a completely appropriate example to use as a beacon for our own spiritual development. We can clearly see a level of realization that such a bodhisattva has that we do not have, but that we are capable of attaining with diligent effort, reliance on the proper spiritual friend, and the proper training.

We should reflect on what prevents us from getting to this point on the path. What keeps us from skillfully working with afflictive emotions and conceptual thoughts the way this bodhisattva does? Though we cannot say so exclusively, we can say that in large part it is our lack of skills in working with mindfulness and discernment.

One of the differences between the Vajrayana and the Causal Vehicle—which is another name, basically, for practicing in accordance with the sutras—is that the Vajrayana teachings present a method that enables a genuine practitioner who has skillfully trained and studied with an authentic master to simultaneously generate an affliction and transform it to wisdom. With diligent, committed practice, the ability to self-liberate leads to the experience of "seeing," equivalent to what the sutras call the *first bhumi*. In other words, having even a glimpse of a bodhisattva's experience of wisdom makes complete realization possible. Taking this example, we can see a way for us to develop the wisdom of a great being like Nagarjuna. Seeing that transformation is possible should empower us to take action. That is the benefit of having a beacon—something to look toward as a source of motivation and inspiration.

Yet it is important to realize that this is not easily done. I am not suggesting that we can work at this intensively for a year or two and then get back to our regular life and expect to be completely transformed. I once met a woman who told me that she wanted to practice a lot for the next year or two so that after that, she could go back to her full time job and lead a normal, American life. But meditation is not like that. Meditation is fruitful when it is lifelong. And it is not something that can be done without the prior training and skills that I am laying out as the foundation for practice.

One of the reasons I wanted to talk about mastery over the mind and mastery over wind energy, as it relates to mindfulness and discernment, is because I think it is important that people who want to be good practitioners know about this connection. We need to have a realistic idea of what the path looks like. When an extraordinary practitioner has an ability or an experience that ordinary people do not have, we also need to have a realistic idea of what that practitioner did to develop that ability or experience, and the reasons that those came about. Then we have a real chance to be the architects of our future. That is the true purpose of meditating on the bodhisattva path. It gives us the chance to take up the ways of skillful compassion, and to transform in ways we never dreamed possible.

Summary

Three methods for training in mindfulness and wind energy:

Train in noticing the karmic breath in the abdomen and chest. Notice what it feels like, and what effect it has on the mind.

Train in dispelling the karmic breath.

Reflect on your own goals for practice as a method for committing to and motivating yourself to practice.

CHAPTER 8

Guards at the Door
to Enlightenment

It has been about 2,500 years since the Buddha Shakya-muni attained enlightenment. After attaining enlighten-ment, he turned the wheel of Dharma three times, which is to say that he gave three different types of Dharma teachings. Among these three turnings of the wheel, there are generally two classi-fications of teachings that are given. One classification is teachings that treat the world, beings, and objects just as they are conven-tionally understood to be. Another includes a style of teachings that talk about the true nature of beings and phenomena. For example, these are the teachings on emptiness, of buddha nature, and the nature of mind. Both of these styles of teachings can be of value to a different kind of practitioner, or to one practitioner at different times.

We can describe these two kinds of teachings by allying them with the two truths. The teachings called *drang don* are given from the point of view of conventional reality, or the ordinary world as we relate to it. The teachings called *ngey don* are given from the point of view of ultimate reality. They need no interpretation because they simply express reality as it is.

The teachings that we have been considering so far have been about mindfulness and discernment from the *drang don* point of view. That is to say, the root verses and scriptures we have been reflecting on all require some kind of interpretation or extra analysis to become a true method for practice. And we should keep in mind that without teachings that require us to analyze and understand conventional reality, it is impossible for us to realize the definitive meaning of the teachings, or ultimate reality.

Usually, when people begin studying the Buddhist teachings it is because they want to know what they call "the truth." This is the implication of the word "suchness" as translated from the Tibetan language. "Truth" is simply another way of saying *what things really are*. That is the "-ness" quality of the word suchness; "-ness" implies the essence of the thing itself. But what happens if we rely upon teachings that do not actually give us a method— teachings that do not give us a way to analyze what the mind does? We have no way to realize "the truth," if we want to call it that. This statement is clearly valid when we think about science and how science comes to understand the world, as science cannot come to conclusions about the nature of phenomena without extensive research into how things function and also how they are interrelated. And it is the same with the mind.

We have been focusing heavily on the mind's discerning quality. We might think, "Why do I have to hear more about discernment? Haven't I gotten it already?" My answer is this: Let us talk about discernment one last time, this time in terms of the very highest teachings in the Nyingma and Kagyu traditions, those of Dzogchen and Mahamudra.

Say that we want to go to the highest floor of any building in the world. What if we wanted to get to the top of that building without taking the stairs? Maybe we could rent a helicopter, hover over the top of the building, and have someone push us out the door. But even if we did that, we would probably injure ourselves in the fall.

No matter what, we have to rely upon something to get to the top. We must have a method. Actually, the idea of being able to soar above everything, high in the sky, and simply drop down is not only impractical in worldly life, but it is not useful in meditation either. How many of us have the courage to jump without having any idea of how and where we will land? It is a much better idea to start at the bottom and work our way up. That way, we can be really sure that what we are doing is leading us to the right place. That is the job of discernment. In Tibet, a particular lama stands out in my mind as being a great master of mindfulness and discernment. I was still young the first time I met him. At that time, he was just an ordinary householder, not wearing robes or dressed in any particularly remarkable manner.

I remember that it was incredible to watch him. He was almost like a stone when he sat. He did not move. Nothing seemed to bother him because his mind was so incredibly stable. I have to be honest; at first, I thought he was conceited and that he was a fake. I thought he just was trying to make everyone think he was a great practitioner. But after I spent more and more time with him, I came to realize that the quality of his mindfulness and discernment were quite profound. He had a distinct quality to him that was unlike that of anyone else. The thing that most impressed me was his consistency. No matter what he did, it always had the same precision. No matter who he spoke to or what he said, how he dressed or how he acted, there was a precision to it all. Later, I realized that an ordinary person cannot achieve this type of incredible precision and mind stability without a profound practice of mindfulness and discernment.

Contrary Purpose?

We might also think, "Isn't training in mindfulness and discernment really a practice of multiplying our thoughts, instead of meditation on the nature of mind, which is the practice of cutting through our conceptual thoughts?" Again, we have to be realistic about what the practice of meditation entails. If we want to be able to abide in the nature of mind or the nature of suchness, we have to rely upon certain techniques in the beginning. It is unrealistic to think that someone, at the beginning, can go from an ordinary state of mind, full of distractions and constant conceptualization, to a state where those things are not present at all. That is a self-defeating expectation.

Many students of the Vajrayana go around receiving all kinds of teachings, and perhaps ones for which they are not well prepared. For example, there is one teaching, a secret oral instruction from the lineage of Patrul Rinpoche called, "The Three Words that Strike the Vital Points." Actually, I have come to realize that this teaching is not so secret in the West, but where I come from, very few monks or nuns are fortunate enough to receive this teaching even once in their lifetimes. Additionally, in Tibet, this teaching is never given without years of preparation beforehand. Ngondro practice is essential, in addition to the serious contemplation and practice of bodhichitta and other basic tenets of the path.

When a practitioner receives this teaching from a master to whom they are uncommonly devoted, and who has the quality of authentic realization, it directly conveys to the practitioner what to "do" when abiding in the nature of mind. Of course, there is nothing to "do" actually, since this word has a dualistic implication, and suggests there is a technique being used. Actually, we say that Dzogchen is the absence of technique and doing. However, because of the constraints of language, I will loosely describe it like this. If we have not trained in mindfulness and discernment prior to receiving this teaching, we would have no idea about what we should do with the instruction.

Without this preparation, it might still be beautiful to hear, of course. We might deepen our faith or receive a blessing as a result of receiving the teaching. But the bottom line is, the teaching would not make any practical sense because this teaching is given with a certain kind of practitioner in mind—a practitioner with a certain level of training.

If we have received this teaching in the past, we should reflect on our experience. Did we really understand the meaning of the teaching? Was our understanding thorough? Is mere "understanding" of the meaning of a teaching sufficient, or is there something beyond conventional understanding to be glimpsed or experienced?

In other words, when we have the chance to reflect on the teachings on mindfulness and discernment, then we actually have the opportunity to develop the skills and foundation necessary to put the highest teachings of Dzogchen into practice. When we do not take that chance, it is regrettable, since we cannot blame anyone but ourselves for this error.

Put in a slightly different manner, what would happen if we received the introduction to the nature of mind with no prior training? We would receive the introduction, but we would have nothing to rely upon in relating to it. We would have no training upon which we could "catch the experience," or enable ourselves to gain a deep, beyond-conventional understanding of that instruction. When the mind lacks stability, a practitioner is simply unable to abide in genuine meditation.

Without developing mindfulness and discernment, we may read or hear about a profound teaching, we may even receive a profound teaching—but the mind is something like a container with a hole in it. If we pour water into such a container, at first it appears to be full. In that same way, I am pretty sure that at first each person probably has at least an intuitive feeling that he or she understands the meaning of the teachings on the nature of mind. But over time, the water leaks out of the container. It cannot remain full.

Just so, after a few days pass, we begin to notice that the initial feeling of understanding we had while the teaching was being transmitted does not get us anywhere. We try to think back to exactly how we felt, and we latch on to that as a precious moment of wisdom—the moment where *we got it, we knew.* But thinking back to such a moment is just attachment. A remembered experience cannot refresh and renew itself. A moment experienced has passed and does not have the quality of life and vitality.

Do not misunderstand the manner of transmission and realization in our profound lineage. Moments of transmission or insight are only meant to be a touchstone, a pointer for what to do in the future or a way to compare the relative authenticity of our later experience. Such moments were never meant to become beautiful, coveted, gilded memories that we keep because we do not know how to enter the experience again. Meditation is an ongoing, fresh experience. It is not a room full of photographs or trinkets to remind us of what we have been through.

Momentary Dharmakaya

I have found it extremely helpful to think of meditation on the nature of mind, that precise moment where mindfulness, discernment, and the expression of wisdom all come together, as the "momentary Dharmakaya." I want to qualify this statement, because actually, from the point of view of the Dharmakaya, there is no separation of anything at all. There is no duality, no this and that. The Dharmakaya is simply the naked experience of the mind's true nature. So, we actually cannot truly call it a "coming together" of mental elements. However, for the purposes of teaching, again, please have patience with the constraints of language.

In this case, we cannot think of what I am talking about as ordinary mindfulness and discernment. The teachings actually call these aspects of the expression of wisdom "effortless mindfulness and discernment" or "the mindfulness and discernment of suchness." As the language tries to point out, mindfulness and discernment at this point become self-arising qualities that enable the mind to abide in the expression of wisdom. Still, it is helpful to reflect on the relationship between the mindfulness and discernment of suchness, and ordinary mindfulness and discernment. Like any other ordinary and extraordinary aspects of practice, mastering the ordinary gives rise to the extraordinary. Again, we see the importance of training in mindfulness and discernment from the beginning.

Actually, we should not understand the Dharmakaya as being a lasting experience at all. I once met a practitioner who said, "The first time I experienced the nature of mind, it lasted for several months." At the same time, however, this practitioner was experiencing ordinary, dualistic mind when he spoke to me. This is a mistaken understanding of the Dharmakaya. If we were able to abide continuously in the Dharmakaya for many months, what would be the reason for later becoming just like an ordinary, afflicted being? If that is our experience, we have misunderstood the Vajrayana teachings. As always, I advocate making an honest self-assessment.

For a buddha, the Dharmakaya is nakedly present in every moment. But for us, the Dharmakaya is fleeting—an expression of energy that is there one moment and gone the next. Without mindfulness and discernment, we will miss it. In fact we do miss it. Each and every moment, we have the opportunity to recognize the momentary Dharmakaya but we fail to do so. We remain stuck in our ordinary minds, overwhelmed by our ordinary habits. This is not meant as discouragement—it is simply meant to make us aware of what we already have the potential to see, but do not.

The momentary Dharmakaya is quite extraordinary. It is the key to what we could call "momentary buddhahood." From the tantric point of view, we do not think of buddhahood as something that happens all at once. Rather, it is a series of moments when the mind recognizes its own luminous nature of clarity and emptiness. At first, these moments are very far apart. But, with diligent practice and training in mindfulness and discernment, these moments come closer and closer together. For an advanced practitioner, they start to blend together—like a dotted line that eventually becomes solid. If we understand the momentary nature of realization, then each moment becomes a great opportunity for us. It is the opportunity for practice, for realization. Each moment is precious, because we have the opportunity to start fresh and to see, nakedly, the Dharmakaya once again and experience a moment of enlightenment.

If we see realization in this way, it fits with the basic understanding we have of the mind. The mind is a continuum, made up of many moments. Some of those moments are pure, some afflicted. It is up to us to change the kinds of moments that dominate our lives.

We have the power to change the mind, fundamentally, at every moment.

The View

When the view of indivisible clarity and emptiness, also described as *rigpa* or "the uncontrived view," arises, it appears for an instant, and then a thought or concept will come and interrupt it. This is basically the same as having an experience of the view that is not clear—it is sort of there, but not really there. Conceptuality happens because we are repeatedly overpowered by the dualistic tendency of the mind. We find that this tendency disrupts our ability to abide in the view. If we are not diligent and we do not constantly work at mindfulness and discernment, then this is just a natural thing that happens. To dispel this tendency, we must work toward mastering mindfulness and discernment, so that both become truly extraordinary.

Maybe it is a bit hard to think about this in terms of the view, but let us think about the same thing in terms of loving-kindness or compassion. When we experience loving-kindness and compassion, it is easy for us to notice it as an instantaneous, genuine, clear experience. We might feel authentic compassion or bodhichitta for a moment.

When we try to extend that compassion and make it continuous, it gets muddled up. Another way to say it is that it loses its clarity. It could be clear in that first moment, but we later see that the experience, as it gets farther and farther away, loses that initial clarity. The view is the same way. I am reminded of the metaphor given earlier about the water that bubbles up from the mouth of the stream, but collects dirt as it travels down the mountain. When the view is present, the energy of clarity and emptiness is present. It is like putting a piece of steel into a fire. The steel gets really hot, turns red, and heat radiates from it. The color, heat, and glow of the steel are indivisible. Yet the longer that we leave that steel out of the fire, the cooler it becomes and it begins to turn gray. Even though it is still hot, it does not have the clear energy of the red glow to it. Once that redness is gone, it begins to turn cold.

We can think of the view in the same way. When that energy is not present, it is like the steel that is starting to become cold. It has lost the indivisible quality of the genuine expression of wisdom. Mindfulness and discernment enable us to recognize the phase of the steel. We should know, not in the sense of intellectually knowing, but in the sense of effortlessly knowing, whether the energy of clarity and emptiness are present. We should know when it is cooling off, so to speak, and when to begin our meditation again.

Actually, the word "effortless" in the Dzogchen teachings as a whole refers to the qualities of mindfulness and discernment. As a result of intensive mind training on the path, a great yogi or siddha has the ability to effortlessly discern and be aware of what is happening in the mind, so that he or she can use a high level of skill and intuitive shifting to abide properly in the nature of mind.

I have said that without training in mindfulness and discernment, and without understanding the way that the momentary Dharmakaya leads to authentic realization over time, we have no way to practice the instructions of our lama. The first reason that this is true is that from the outset, the mind lacks stability. Without the basis of stability, the wind energy is easily agitated and the mind cannot settle and relax, not to mention abide in the nature of mind. When the mind is agitated, we fail to practice anything but putting out the fire that has been ignited and gotten out of control.

Always remember that effortless mindfulness and discernment are what enable us to experience the nature of mind, even for an instant. It covers up all the holes in the bottom of the container so that we are able to rest in the view.

If we lack mindfulness, we will not remember what we were taught, and we will forget the meaning of the teachings. Without discernment, we will not know when to practice—Please internalize these words until you believe them with all of your heart. If you remember and practice these instructions, you will be able to master the pith instructions.

Our minds are the doors to enlightenment. Each and every individual has buddha nature, the possibility of true realization. Each and every being has access to the momentary Dharmakaya and can experience momentary buddhahood. We have the potential to enter and abide in these experiences because we have ordinary, discursive mind. Think of discernment as the guard outside the door, watching who is coming in. Think of mindfulness as the guard inside the door, watching what is going on inside the mind, seeing who has come through the door. Without guards on either side of the door, thieves will steal in and take everything that is valuable.

Those thieves are the wolf-like afflictive emotions, always watching and waiting for an opportunity to feed. We have to guard against the afflictive emotions and the mind's contaminated, habitual qualities, or the wolf will devour our potential, and the thieves will steal any undistracted moment or peaceful quality in the mind.

The door of the mind must always be protected by the two guards of mindfulness and discernment. If either one is missing it will be easy for the afflictive emotions to come in the door and steal away the experience of meditation.

What Makes Realization Possible?

What is it that makes realization possible? This is not a simple question, and if we think it is mindfulness and discernment, we would not be wrong. But what else is necessary? Is it incredible intelligence or an outstanding disposition for Dharma practice? Is it simply the karmic connections we have made in the past that are ripening? These things might help, but actually what fuels realization is the practice of abiding in the genuine experience of meditation, over and over again. We have to experience moments of nakedly abiding in the nature of mind, the momentary Dharmakaya, over and over again. Of course, that is why we call meditation "practice."

Without the basis of listening and contemplation, we will not be able to abide in the momentary Dharmakaya even once—not to mention hundreds and thousands of times. This is why our knowledge and our experience diverge rather than converge. When we cannot bring knowledge and experience together, real- ization is impossible. Mindfulness and discernment can act as the bridge between them.

When I was younger and first learning about Buddhist phi- losophy in earnest, there was a time when I did not really feel like making the effort to master the foundational teachings. To be honest, I did not really feel like studying logic or Madhyamika, as I was really keen on the tantras. Later, after a lot of urging from my root lama, my personality changed. Out of devotion to my lama, I generated a deep aspiration to master the entire lineage of teachings, including the foundational teachings. This is true even though at that time, I did not understand the benefit of doing so. And yet, now, I can share with you what I learned from that experience.

When I compare my experience of meditation during the time I did not study diligently to the time when I did, it is very easy for me to see that when I finally began delving into the foundational teachings and Madhyamika, I became more grounded in the Dharma, so to speak. My meditation improved exponentially. It was quite incredible, actually. Working through any resistance we might have to mastering the entire canon of teachings is a worthwhile thing to do. From where we are now, we might not be able to see the difference. But with some perspective, and seeing the positive changes that come over the mind as a result of focused mind training, we can be grateful for the change of direction.

A Profound Transmission

When I was nineteen years old, my root lama gave me a very special transmission of *The Treasury of the Dharmadhatu*, which is a wonderful teaching by Longchenpa, one of the texts included in the profound collection called the *Seven Treasures*. After my lama gave me this teaching, I felt that there was no point in studying other things. I felt that *this was it*. So I went to my lama and said, "I want to stay in retreat for the rest of my life. I received this

teaching and this is all I want to practice for the rest of my life."
I thought my lama would be very happy that I was so serious
about one teaching.

What do you expect my root lama did? He was ever-changing,
depending on the circumstances and what I needed from him at
the moment. Sometimes he was fierce and wrathful, and sometimes incredibly soft and gentle. But on this day, my lama just
burst out laughing. He said, "Do you think you are going to be
able to practice that text without any other experience and training whatsoever? Do you think you realized that text just because
you heard it and you feel like you understood it? Is that the same
thing as realization?"

Then my lama said, very seriously, "Without serious training
beforehand, what you are proposing would not be a 'retreat.' It
would simply be a wild person in a wild place, staying in a wild
cave, drinking wild water, with no understanding of how to tame
the mind properly. How will a person like you be able to stay out
in the wilderness and practice for the rest of your life?" My lama
advised me to stay and study and gain a good foundation in meditation so that I would be able to realize those teachings in the
future, and practice authentically in retreat.

When I reflect back, I realize that I had no mindfulness and no
discernment at that young age. I had no idea what I was planning
to do, or what a lifelong practice would entail when I said those
words. I was also very arrogant when I was young, and it was
humbling to be told that I should stay at Shedra, the tantric university where I lived, and study more.

It is not a fault to love profound Dharma teachings. Actually, it
is good for our aspirations as Dharma practitioners to love the
profound teachings of Dzogchen and Mahamudra—it helps us

to have genuine faith that enlightenment is possible, and that we have the potential to become enlightened if only we practice properly. I love these teachings, too. However, I want to remind you how important it is not to neglect the initial teachings that make precious and marvelous teachings meaningful, and the realization of them possible.

Reflect on the difference between looking at the sky and directly seeing the sun, and seeing the reflection of the sun in a pool of water. Those are very different things. If we lack the proper foundation, looking directly at the sun is impossible. The only thing we can do is look at the reflection of the sun in a pool of water; that is the closest we can get to genuine experience.

But I can say with certainty that after we work at mind training enthusiastically, one day we will be able to look at the sun—and that will be a truly incredible experience. You will not have to take my word for what this experience is like, because it will be something you know directly.

That is a wish I make here for you, and for all sentient beings!

> May all beings see the beautiful light rays
> of the mind's radiant luminosity,
> and never be satisfied by simply seeing
> the reflection of the sun in the water!

About the Author

Anyen Rinpoche is part of an unbroken lineage who received the Longchen Nyingthig and Dzogchen teachings directly from the renowned Dzogchen master Patrul Rinpoche. Rinpoche is known throughout the world for his profound comprehension of the Dharma as well as his easy-to-understand teaching style. He has taught extensively in Tibet and China and now mentors students throughout Southeast Asia, Japan, and North America. He is the author of *The Union of Dzogchen and Bodhichitta*, and is the founder of Orgyen Khamdroling Sangha in Denver, Colorado, where he now lives.

About the Editor/Translator

Allison Graboski is a student of Anyen Rinpoche and his root master, Tsara Dharmakirti Rinpoche. She has been studying Tibetan language and Buddhism under Anyen Rinpoche's guidance for the past nine years. She is Anyen Rinpoche's personal translator for both dharma talks and textual translations. She lives in Denver, Colorado.

Wisdom Publications

Wisdom Publications, a nonprofit publisher, is dedicated to making available authentic Buddhist works for the benefit of all. We publish translations of the sutras and tantras, commentaries and teachings of past and contemporary Buddhist masters, and original works by the world's leading Buddhist scholars. We publish our titles with the appreciation of Buddhism as a living philosophy and with the special commitment to preserve and transmit important works from all the major Buddhist traditions.

To learn more about Wisdom, or to browse books online, visit our website at wisdompubs.org. You may request a copy of our mail-order catalog online or by writing to this address:

Wisdom Publications
199 Elm Street
Somerville, Massachusetts 02144 USA
Telephone: (617) 776-7416
Fax: (617) 776-7841
Email: info@wisdompubs.org
www.wisdompubs.org

The Wisdom Trust

As a nonprofit publisher, Wisdom is dedicated to the publication of fine Dharma books for the benefit of all sentient beings and is dependent upon the kindness and generosity of sponsors in order to do so. If you would like to make a donation to Wisdom, please do so through our Somerville office. If you would like to sponsor the publication of a book, please write or email us at the address above.

Thank you.

Wisdom is a nonprofit, charitable 501(c)(3) organization affiliated with the Foundation for the Preservation of the Mahayana Tradition (FPMT).